Succeed in LanguageCert Expert CEFR Level C1 ESOL/SELT 朗思全真模拟题

（英）安德鲁·贝蒂斯（Andrew Betsis）
（英）劳伦斯·马马斯（Lawrence Mamas） 编著

华中科技大学出版社
http://press.hust.edu.cn
中国·武汉

图书在版编目（CIP）数据

朗思全真模拟题＝Succeed in LanguageCert Expert CEFR Level C1 ESOL/SELT：英文／（英）安德鲁·贝蒂斯,（英）劳伦斯·马马斯编著. — 武汉：华中科技大学出版社，2022.12
ISBN 978-7-5680-8887-9

Ⅰ.①朗… Ⅱ.①安… ②劳… Ⅲ.①英语水平考试—习题集 Ⅳ.① H310.41-44

中国版本图书馆 CIP 数据核字 (2022) 第 238256 号

湖北省版权局著作权合同登记 图字：17-2022-142 号

朗思全真模拟题 Succeed in LanguageCert Expert CEFR Level C1 ESOL/SELT　　（英）安德鲁·贝蒂斯
　　　　　　　　　　　　　　　　　　　　　　　　　　　　　　　　　　　（英）劳伦斯·马马斯　编著

策划编辑：熊元勇　阮　钊　傅　文　李娟娟
责任编辑：傅　文　马红静
封面设计：郎思哥
责任校对：刘小雨
责任监印：朱　玢
出版发行：华中科技大学出版社（中国·武汉）　　　　电　话：（027）81321913
　　　　　武汉市东湖新技术开发区华工科技园　　　　邮　编：430223
录　　排：华中科技大学惠友文印中心
印　　刷：武汉市籍缘印刷厂
开　　本：787 mm×1092 mm　1/16
印　　张：11.75
字　　数：217 千字
版　　次：2022 年 12 月第 1 版第 1 次印刷
定　　价：88.00 元

本书若有印装质量问题，请向出版社营销中心调换
全国免费服务热线：400-6679-118　　竭诚为您服务
版权所有　侵权必究

Contents

No. 1
Practice Paper Tests

Practice Paper Test 1 002

Practice Paper Test 2 024

Practice Paper Test 3 045

Practice Paper Test 4 067

Practice Paper Test 5 089

No. 2
Speaking Tests ESOL

Test 1 112

Test 2 119

Test 3 126

Test 4 133

Test 5 140

No. 3
Audio Scripts

Test 1 148

Test 2 154

Test 3 160

Test 4 166

Test 5 173

About LanguageCert English Spoken Other Language (ESOL) Test 180

Answer Key 181

No.1

Practice Paper Tests

LanguageCert
Expert C1
Level 2
International ESOL (Listening, Reading, Writing)
Practice Paper Test 1

Listening Test Audio

Candidate's name (block letters please)

Centre no   **Date**

Time allowed:

Listening	about 30 minutes
Reading and Writing	2 hours and 40 minutes

Instructions to Candidates

- An Answer Sheet will be provided.

- All answers must be transferred to the Answer Sheet.

- Please use a softpencil (2B, HB).

Listening Part 1

You will hear six short, unfinished conversations. Choose the **best reply** to continue each conversation. Put a circle round the letter of the **best reply**. Look at the example. You will hear each conversation **twice**.

Example:
Speaker 1: Is this the right size?
Speaker 2: I think it's OK.
Speaker 1: We should have checked the size before we had bought it.
Speaker 2: ....
        a) Why do you ask?
      (b) You are right, but it's too late now.
        c) I've checked the shop.

1. a) What do you mean? Like what?
   b) But really, isn't it always?
   c) I am not acting.

2. a) I had no idea.
   b) I thought the shops were closed.
   c) Maybe I will go shopping later.

3. a) Inside out.
   b) My parents' house.
   c) I bought the aspirin at the pharmacy.

4. a) It isn't here.
   b) I doubt it.
   c) It's an awful colour.

5. a) I will if you do, too.
   b) Must you though?
   c) Do you really?

6. a) I have no idea.
   b) You know where she is now?
   c) It's no use wandering around.

Listening Part 2

You will hear three conversations. Listen to the conversations and answer the questions. Put a circle round the letter of the correct answer. You will hear each conversation **twice**. Look at the questions for Conversation One.

Conversation 1

1. Why was the woman in America?
   a) to work
   b) to travel
   c) to meet friends

2. The man has
   a) travelled a lot.
   b) lived in one place for a long time.
   c) never been out of his country.

Conversation 2

3. The woman is
   a) a school advisor.
   b) a student.
   c) a politician.

4. What does the man want?
   a) school credit
   b) to find a band
   c) to be called back by Friday

Conversation 3

5. The relationship between the man and the woman is
   a) husband and wife.
   b) computer technician and client.
   c) salesperson and customer.

6. The woman
   a) does not have a DVD playing programme on her computer.
   b) doesn't like the DVD programme the man wants to sell her.
   c) doesn't like her current DVD programme.

No.1 Practice Paper Tests

Listening Part 3

Listen to the person talking and complete the information on the notepad. Write **short** answers of one to five words. You will hear the person **twice**. At the end you will have two minutes to read through and check your answers. You have one minute to look at the notepad. The first one is an example.

DO NOT WRITE MORE THAN 5 WORDS FOR EACH QUESTION.

"Processing the Work of The Secret Government"

Example:

Film informs people of: *U.S. government's operations*

1. The 2 enemies in the proxy war:
   ....

2. Country the Contras were expected to fight:
   ....

3. Name of group formed by private donors:
   ....

4. Focus of the documentary:
   ....

5. Political fact in Guatemala documentary:
   ....

6. What the US dominated in the Caribbean:
   ....

7. A scandal the film deals with:
   ....

Listening Part 4

Listen to the conversation and answer the questions. Put a circle round the letter of the correct answer. An example is done for you. You will hear the conversation **twice**.

Example: What has the woman just finished?
    a) writing her first book
    (b) writing a new book
    c) reading a new book

1. For what age groups has Judy Blume written books?

    a) only for children

    b) mostly for teenagers

    c) for all age groups

2. What is the main character, in Judy Blume's new novel, obsessed with?

    a) money

    b) time

    c) friends

3. The name of Judy Blume's grandson is

    a) Peter.

    b) Howie.

    c) Elliot.

4. How does Judy Blume feel about being a grandmother?

    a) It helps her remember childhood.

    b) It gives her a new way to look at childhood.

    c) It helps her stay in touch with young people.

5. How does Judy Blume start writing a book?

   a) She writes a first draft very quickly.

   b) She keeps a notebook with ideas in it.

   c) She writes several drafts very slowly.

6. Before Judy sends her books to her editor,

   a) she reads it aloud.

   b) she asks the opinion of her editor.

   c) she asks her family's opinion.

7. What part of writing does Judy Blume find difficult?

   a) developing characters

   b) her last draft

   c) her first draft

Reading Part 1

Read the following text, then read the five statements. Some of these statements are true according to the text, some of them are false. Write T for True or F for False in the box next to each statement.

In the simple example of a college graduation ceremony, the liminal phase can actually be extended to include the period of time between when the last assignment was finished (and graduation was assured) all the way through reception of the diploma. That no man's land represents the limbo associated with liminality. The stress of accomplishing tasks for college has been lifted. Yet, the individual has not  transitioned to a new stage in life (psychologically or physically). The result is a unique perspective on what has come before, and what may come next.

When Western cultures use mistletoe, the plant is placed in a threshold (the "limen"), at the time of the winter solstice. The act that occurs under the mistletoe (the kiss) breaks the boundaries between two people. Because what happens under the mistletoe is occurring in ritual time/space, the people kissing are not breaking taboos imposed under normal circumstances by their marriages to (or relationships with) other people. When a marriage proposal is initiated, there is a liminal stage between the question and the answer during which the social arrangements of both parties involved are subject to transformation and inversion; a sort of "life stage limbo" so to speak, in that the affirmation or denial can result in multiple and diverse outcomes.

Twilight serves as a liminal time, between day and night. The name of the television fiction series *The Twilight Zone* makes reference to this, describing it as "the middle ground between light and shadow, between science and superstition" in one variant of the original series' opening. The name is from an actual zone observable from space in the place where daylight or shadow advances or retreats about the Earth. Noon and, more often, midnight can be considered liminal, the first transitioning between morning and afternoon, the latter between days.

1. Liminality is a word used to describe certain stages in life. ☐
2. Liminality is a transitional period. ☐
3. People kissing is representative of liminality. ☐
4. Rejection of a marriage proposal can lead to depression. ☐
5. The television show *The Twilight Zone* coined the term "liminality". ☐

Reading Part 2

Read the text and fill the gaps with the correct sentences A-H. Write the letter of the missing sentence in the box in the gap. There are two extra sentences you will not need.

Marwell Zoo

Marwell Zoological Park, or Marwell Zoo, is situated in Hampshire, England, near Winchester. **1** It is best known for its large collection of ungulates and unique style of enclosures. Marwell Zoological Park is owned and operated by the Marwell Preservation Trust, a registered charity.

The zoo's logo is a silhouetted oryx. The oryx was one of the first species kept at Marwell and more than 200 calves have been born and reared there since 1972. London, Whipsnade and Edinburgh Zoos cooperate with Marwell's oryx breeding programme, which aims to reintroduce the animal to its natural habitat. **2**

In the eight years preceding their arrival an area of 24 square kilometres had been kept free from habitation, grazing and cultivation, resulting in a dramatic recovery of vegetation, and provision of a perfect reintroduction site for the captive-born oryx. **3**

The Zoological Park exists in the manor of Marwell. Marwell Hall is a Grade I listed building and was once the residence of Sir Henry Seymour (brother of Jane Seymour, Henry VIII's third wife) so it is likely that Henry visited on several occasions. **4**

In 1977, a giraffe called Victor collapsed on his stomach, and was unable to get up. **5** All attempts to get him on his feet failed, and his plight became a major international news story. The Royal Navy were brought in, and made a sling to winch him onto his feet. He died of a heart attack very shortly afterwards. The publicity turned Marwell into a major tourist attraction, and interest was revived the following summer, when Victor's mate, Dribbles, gave birth to a female calf, Victoria.

In 1999, the zoo lost all 26 of its Jackass and Macaroni Penguins to avian malaria. **6** After consulting with various experts, the exhibit was restocked with Humboldt Penguins, which are present in greater numbers in captivity (although endangered in the wild).

A. In December 1985 ten yearling oryx were transferred from Marwell to the Bou-Hedma National Park in Tunisia (part of the former range of their ancestors).

B. The press claimed that he had slipped while trying to mate.

C. Since 1985, the herd has settled in well, has started to breed, and has become increasingly wary of humans.

D. There were other cases in the UK but Marwell was the only zoo to lose its entire colony, which had arrived only two and a half years before.

E. Though no major exhibits will be opening in 2018, the zoo is opening a new Giant Anteater house and enclosure to form part of the new South American biome in 2019.

F. Following a replacement, the first cub born to the new pair escaped into the male's enclosure through a partition and was killed.

G. There is a local tale that they were married in a private ceremony, either at the hall, or in nearby Owslebury, very soon after news arrived from London confirming the death of Anne Boleyn.

H. Opened in 1972, it was one of the earliest zoos in Europe to place an emphasis on animal conservation and is considered one of the leading institutions in that field.

Reading Part 3

Read the four texts below. There are eight questions about the texts. Decide which text (A, B, C or D) tells you the answer to the question. The first one is done for you.

A.

The idea that bars will be forced to close because of the smoking ban is utterly unconvincing. In other cities where smoking bans were enacted, post-ban bar profits went up. There are more people unwilling to go into the smoke-filled bars as they exist today than there are smokers unwilling to go into smoke-free areas.

It is also foolhardy to assert that smokers who light up in bars would choose not to frequent the smokeless bars. Smoking, like television, is an activity that can be done at home, at any time. Listening to live music is the real draw of the bar scene - not ubiquitous cigarettes- and someone who'd miss out on listening to Austin's live music because they'd rather stay home and light up a cigarette is a pretty sad sack.

B.

As a non-smoker, when the smoking ban was first proposed, the prospect of being able to eat a meal or have a drink with some friends without being drowned in the off-putting smell of smoke was wonderful. It was only when I started to look at the specifics that I realised that perhaps this ban wasn't entirely ethical and good willed.

C.

I genuinely believe that over the past few years, smokers have become more understanding and considerate to our rightly health-conscious society and the question "do you mind if I light up?" is more prominent than ever.

As a student, much of my social life is spent with friends in both bars and restaurants. Those of my friends who do smoke have become more accustomed to "smoke free" or "smoking areas" within these establishments. The non-smokers amongst us have also become used to these disciplines.

I believe that by being tolerant of each other's rights to enjoy a relaxing social life, we should be able to avoid the need of an unfair ban that affects smokers and non-smokers alike.

D.

I feel that this impinges upon people's rights and no one should be forced to give up something they don't want to. Personal health and safety has to do with the individual - not the public.

Passive smoking is the same as car-fume inhalation, just a little lighter on the lungs, but the long-term effects are just as prominent; it is just so idiotic and not sensible. Ancient Indians smoked the pipe as do the modern eastern Islamic countries and is part of a tradition and yet, why aren't they being banned when they equally contain just as many powerful toxins that are inhaled and exhaled as regular cigarettes?

In which text does the writer:

Example: argue that smoking is a tradition that shouldn't be banned? <u>D</u>

1. claim smokers have recently become more respectful?
2. hint a smoking ban may lack moral basis?
3. argue that bars won't be affected by a smoking ban?

Which text is saying the following?

4. An individual's well-being is private.
5. Smokers and non-smokers need to respect each other.
6. In some places, establishments made more money after a smoking ban was passed.
7. At first the thought of a smoking ban was nice.

Reading Part 4

Read the article and answer the questions. **Write a maximum of five words for each answer**. An example is done for you.

Intelligence

While showing an impressive growth prenatally, the human brain is not fully formed at birth. There is considerable brain growth during childhood with dynamic changes taking place in the human brain throughout life, probably for adaptation to our environment.

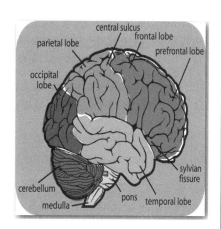

Defining intelligence is highly problematic. Is there an "intelligence" that equips us to solve all kinds of problems and answer all questions, regardless of their nature? Or are there different intelligences that help us deal with particular problems and solutions? The scientific community is divided on the issue.

One of the main tenets underpinning the idea of a single entity of "intelligence" is the concept of "General Intelligence", or "g". Devised by English Psychologist, Charles Spearman, in the early 20th century, "g" was a statistical measure of performance across a variety of tests.

Spearman found that the same people who did well in a variety of mental tests tended to use a part in their brains that he termed "g". This "g" laid the foundation for the notion of a single intelligence, which enables us to undertake everyday mental tasks.

A recent study seems to endorse Spearman's theory. Research has found that a part of the brain called the "lateral prefrontal cortex" is the only area of the brain to increase in blood flow when volunteers tackle complicated puzzles.

Spearman's concept, however, is still highly controversial with many people questioning both the statistical process and the simplistic nature of "g". There is also a body of research that states that our mental ability is a function of social factors such as education and not one's inherent biological make-up.

The early Greeks thought the brain was the seat of your soul, rather than your intellect. They believed that thinking happened somewhere around the lungs! Not until the seventeenth century was the brain seen as an organ of intelligence and thought, when the concept of the mind emerged.

There are a number of different methods which purport to measure intelligence, the most famous of which is perhaps the IQ, or "Intelligence Quotient" test. The "Stanford-Binet Intelligence Scale" began life in early 20th-century Paris, as part of Alfred Binet's efforts to educate children with learning difficulties. Those that obtained a score below their age were considered "retarded".

IQ is a "psychometric" test, meaning it measures mental ability. However, defining intelligence is far from simple. There are two main schools of thought. The first believes in an inherited, genetically determined intellect that can be measured. The second group of psychologists believe in many intelligences, the development of which may be the result of our social background. They also think that measuring these intelligences is also problematic. This issue is ongoing and will be studied for years to come, but for now there is no clear way to truly measure intelligence.

No.1 Practice Paper Tests

Example: Why does the human brain change dynamically throughout life?
................................for adaptation to our environment................................

1. How does the author initially describe the process of defining intelligence?

   ....

2. On what research was Spearman's theory based?

   ....

3. Which is the only area of the brain that increases in blood flow when volunteers tackle complicated puzzles?

   ....

4. What aspect of our mental ability cannot be explained by Spearman's theory?

   ....

5. When was the brain seen as an organ of intelligence and thought?

   ....

6. For what category of children was the "Stanford-Binet Intelligence Scale" first devised?

   ....

7. What do IQ tests measure?

   ....

8. Where is the progress of our intelligence based on, according to the second group of psychologists?

   ....

Writing Part 1

You are the Principal of a secondary school and are concerned about the increase of obesity in your students. A local fitness group, called 'Fighting Fit' has offered to conduct a course of fitness classes at your school at a discounted rate for student groups. Using the results of the survey write a **letter** to parents to highlight the need for students to take part in the classes and explain how students will benefit from so doing.

Write between 150 and 200 words.

Fighting Fit!

Classes for kids who don't 'do' fitness.

We make exercise fun for children. If your child is a bit overweight we can make him or her, fit and healthy! Your child will love our fitness classes and adventure assault courses! Don't delay, subscribe today!

Survey into rates of child obesity
(shown as a percentage of the population in the UK)

Age of child	Year 1981-1984	Year 2015-2016
2-5 years	5% obese	13.9% obese
6-11 years	4% obese	18.8% obese
12-19 years	6.1% obese	17.4% obese

Report showing consequences of child obesity:

* 24% of children who are obese report experiencing low self-esteem

* 17% of obese children are at risk of developing Type II diabetes as adults

* 63% of children who are obese, experience bullying at school

* 76% of obese children report experiencing stigma for being obese

Writing Part 2

Write a **composition** describing how someone has changed your life, for better or for worse, and how this will affect your life and attitude to this person.

Write between 250 and 300 words.

LanguageCert
Expert C1
Level 2
International ESOL (Listening, Reading, Writing)
Practice Paper Test 2

Listening Test Audio

Candidate's name (block letters please)

Centre no   **Date**

Time allowed:

Listening   about 30 minutes

Reading and Writing   2 hours and 40 minutes

Instructions to Candidates

- An Answer Sheet will be provided.

- All answers must be transferred to the Answer Sheet.

- Please use a softpencil (2B, HB).

Listening Part 1

You will hear six short, unfinished conversations. Choose the **best reply** to continue each conversation. Put a circle round the letter of the **best reply**. Look at the example. You will hear each conversation **twice**.

Example:
Speaker 1: Is this the right size?
Speaker 2: I think it's OK.
Speaker 1: We should have checked the size before we had bought it.
Speaker 2: ....
    a) Why do you ask?
    (b) You are right, but it's too late now.
    c) I've checked the shop.

1. a) I can't tell you anything.
   b) Why on earth not?
   c) Will you? How's that?

2. a) I hadn't figured it out.
   b) Sometimes I want to arrive early.
   c) Of course! We all did.

3. a) We like you more than you think.
   b) It was fun to see you, too.
   c) Not so great these days.

4. a) It isn't here; I've already checked.
   b) In the bin, I reckon.
   c) It looks OK now.

5. a) I'll check if it's out of stock.

   b) But of course there is! Don't worry!

   c) There might not be; you never know.

6. a) I can't now. It's too late.

   b) It doesn't have to.

   c) I left you some presents.

No.1 Practice Paper Tests

Listening Part 2

You will hear three conversations. Listen to the conversations and answer the questions. Put a circle round the letter of the correct answer. You will hear each conversation **twice**. Look at the questions for Conversation One.

Conversation 1

1. What does the man want the woman to do?

    a) get her work published

    b) start writing a journal

    c) read a paper

2. The woman is the man's

    a) student.

    b) friend.

    c) teacher.

Conversation 2

3. The woman changed her mind about

    a) her husband opening his own pub.

    b) working in a pub.

    c) investing in another pub.

4. The woman wants

    a) the man to be happy.

    b) to work in the pub.

    c) to run the pub herself.

Conversation 3

5. Why is the man angry?
   a) His professor didn't give him back his test.
   b) He couldn't study hard for a test.
   c) He didn't do well on a test.

6. The woman suggests the man
   a) study harder.
   b) talk to his professor.
   c) do better on the next test.

Listening Part 3

Listen to the person talking and complete the information on the notepad. Write **short** answers of one to five words. You will hear the person **twice**. At the end you will have two minutes to read through and check your answers. You have one minute to look at the notepad. The first one is an example.

DO NOT WRITE MORE THAN 5 WORDS FOR EACH QUESTION.

NOTES on Flower Gifting

Example:

Guest: Caitlin Butler

1. Reasons for the existence of variations in flower-gifting:
   ....

2. Two festivals for flower gifting:
   ....

3. One formal occasion flowers are appropriate as a gift:
   ....

4. Peonies - popular wedding gift in:
   ....

5. Inappropriate gifts in Asia:
   ....

6. Flowers signifying death in England:
   ....

7. Number meaning bad luck in Italy:
   ....

Listening Part 4

Listen to the conversation and answer the questions. Put a circle round the letter of the correct answer. An example is done for you. You will hear the conversation **twice**.

Example: Why doesn't the woman understand global warming?

a) It is too much to process.

b) It is too scientific.

c) She is taking a class on it.

1. What is the relationship between El Nino and global warming?

    a) They are the same thing.

    b) They are interrelated.

    c) They have nothing to do with each other.

2. What does the man think about global warming?

    a) It is a real problem and we must take action.

    b) It is a problem for the future generations to solve.

    c) Only scientists believe it is real.

3. When will the effects of today's pollution be evident in the atmosphere?

    a) in 10 years

    b) in 20 years

    c) now

4. The main cause of global warming is

    a) the burning of fossil fuels.

    b) deforestation.

    c) urbanisation.

5. What needs to be done according to UN's scientists?

   a) to cut CO_2 emissions by 60% at once

   b) to cut CO_2 emissions gradually by 60%

   c) to cut CO_2 emissions by at least 7%

6. The US has agreed to

   a) to reduce CO_2 emissions by 70% from 1990 levels.

   b) to reduce CO_2 emissions by 7% from 1990 levels.

   c) to reduce CO_2 emissions by 60% from 1990 levels.

7. What planet has a "runaway green house effect"?

   a) Earth

   b) Venus

   c) Mars

Reading Part 1

Read the following text, then read the five statements. Some of these statements are true according to the text, some of them are false. Write T for True or F for False in the box next to each statement.

In Japan, because the school year begins in April, the graduation ceremony usually occurs in early March. Third-year Senior High School students (equivalent to 12th grade in Canada and the United States) take their finals in early February, so they are able to pass entrance examinations in universities

prior to graduation. This break may contribute to the emotional charge of the event.

Although Japanese schools differ greatly in size (from a mere dozen to thousands of students), the nature of the graduation ceremony itself remains similar. It usually takes place in the school auditorium or agora, or for poorer schools, in the gymnasium. Special drapes, curtains and scrolls are hung to the walls and doors. A certain number of chairs are reserved for parents (usually mothers) to come, as well as local officials. The students do not wear robes or mortarboards. Depending on the school, they might have to buy and wear a one-time only graduation uniform. Most of the time they simply wear their regular school uniform.

At first, all students from the 1st and 2nd grades (equivalent to 10th or 11th grade) wait. Then the graduates march in to the sound of a classical march, often rendered by the school's brass band. A complex series of announcements are made, which cue the students to stand up, bow, sit down. The homeroom teacher for each class calls out the names of his or her students in the usual gender-split alphabetical order. This means that boys are called out in alphabetical order first, then the girls. Upon hearing their names, the students say "Hai" or "Yes" and remain at attention until all students have been called. Recently some schools have discontinued splitting the class by gender. Both the national anthem and school song are sung by everyone. The head of the student council reads a short congratulatory address to the graduates. This is different from a valedictorian speech. Unlike a valedictorian's speech, it is somewhat preset and heavily edited by the teachers responsible for the ceremony.

Afterwards, the principal launches into a long-winded speech as is the tradition in most schools. Perseverance, hard work and patience are the most common themes brought up on the occasion. The principal might wear a full tuxedo, complete with handkerchief and white gloves. The student's ID number and name are read out loud, the diploma is handed over in full size (not rolled-up). The student receives it with both hands, raises it up in the air and bows to the principal before leaving the stage. There can be background music playing in the meantime, either from tape or CD, or provided by the school's brass band.

1. Japanese students take their finals early in the calendar year. ☐
2. Japanese graduation ceremonies always take place in gymnasiums. ☐
3. Often boys have their names called out before girls. ☐
4. The principal sings the school song alone. ☐
5. The principal usually dresses casually at Japanese graduation ceremonies. ☐

Reading Part 2

Read the text and fill the gaps with the correct sentences A-H. Write the letter of the missing sentence in the box in the gap. There are two extra sentences you will not need.

Ska

In 1962, a time when Jamaica was copying the musical style of America, Cecil Bustamente Campbell, later known as Prince Buster, felt that something new was needed. He had his guitarist Jah Jerry emphasise the afterbeat instead of the downbeat. To present day, the afterbeat is essential to Jamaican syncopation. Another artist, Rosco Gordon, is credited with the development of Ska. **1** ☐ So, Ska was born.

2 ☐ One day he was trying to get the guitars to play something, and he started saying 'make the guitars go Ska! , Ska!, Ska!' And that's the way the ska name was used for the first time.

3 ☐ At the same time portable dance music operators running 'Sound Systems' competed for public popularity. The sound system war escalated to the point that people were sent to competitor sound system parties to cause problems and fight. **4** ☐

Throughout the 1960s the ghetto areas of Jamaica were filling up with youths looking for work that did not exist. **5** ☐ These youths drew group identity as 'Rude Boys'. The way the Rude Boys danced the ska was different as well: slower with a menacing posture. The Rude Boys connected with the underworld, those who lived outside the law, and this was reflected in the lyrics of the music. Ska music once again changed to reflect the mood of the rude with more tension in the bass, as opposed to the previous free-walking bass style.

Ska went to England with the immigrants of the early 1960's and was initially known as 'Bluebeat'. This was considered the second wave of Ska. **6** It was recorded in England in 1964 for *Island Records* and featured a young English Mod, Rod Stewart, just beginning his own music career on *Harmonica*. Ska gained popularity amongst the Mod scene.

Recently ska has enjoyed another wave of popularity. The third wave exists in many forms and combines many different styles of rock with ska rhythms and instrumentation.

A. These people were known as 'Dance Hall Crashers'.

B. Soon, growing radio audiences led to the birth of the Jamaican recording industry.

C. Despite such primitive recording facility, ska became the national music of Jamaica.

D. They felt excluded and did not share the optimism of early Ska roots.

E. The first person to record this 'ska' rhythm was Ernest Ranglin when performing with Cluet Johnson and the Blues Busters.

F. Around 1966 the beat of ska was slowed and rocksteady was born.

G. He heavily stressed the second and fourth beats of each bar.

H. The first international ska hit was 'My Boy Lollipop' by Millie Small.

Reading Part 3

Read the four texts below. There are eight questions about the texts. Decide which text (A, B, C or D) tells you the answer to the question. The first one is done for you.

A.

Yes, mobile phones are a big distraction while driving, but I don't think that banning them will change much. First off, many people will still use them while driving because it would be very difficult to stop every person who talks on their phone. Secondly, there are many more things that distract people while driving just as much as phones do. A good example of this now would be MP3 players. So many people use them in the car and are constantly looking at the screen to find a song to play. Or take food as another example. I mean, how many people eat while they drive every day? So, to become a safer driving society, banning mobile phones isn't really the answer. I don't really know what the answer is, but mobile phones are just one issue on the list of deadly distractions in the car.

B.

People should only use mobile phones for emergencies while driving. Earpieces are definitely a good thing to have because then you can keep both hands on the wheel while talking on the phone. You should only use a mobile phone in the car for business and emergency purposes. It is as simple as that.

C.

I don't think mobile phones should be banned. I won't lie about it; I'm guilty of being distracted while driving due to talking on my mobile phone, but it's a personal decision. It kind of upsets me that they've banned mobile phone usage for teens in some places. Teens are not the only ones that get distracted.

D.

I'm pretty sure if the cop sees you eating or putting make up on, if appropriate, would caution you or give you a ticket. It's dangerous driving.

The big thing about banning using your handheld phone while driving, is that giving big fines is not enough. There has to be social pressure saying "It's not cool". Just like as it is with drunk-driving. In the UK you get 3 points on your licence (12 disqualifies) and a £30 fine. Apparently that wasn't a big enough deterrent, and now they are talking about an £1,000 fine, but people use their mobile phones less because other drivers look at you with scorn.

If you are important enough, people can wait for you to call them back when you arrive, or pull the hell over while you have to talk. One life is already too many to lose because someone "had to" make that call.

In which text does the writer

Example: argue just giving fines for talking on mobile phones while driving is not enough?   **D**

1. express that talking on the phone while driving should be a decision made by the individual?

2. argue that ear pieces are a good idea?

3. claim that there are other electronic devices, too, that distract people while driving?

Which text is saying the following?

4. There needs to be a social change to deter people from talking on mobile phones while driving.

5. It is unfair that some people are specifically targeted by the law.

6. Banning mobile phones in cars won't make a big difference.

7. People should use mobile phones when driving only when it is absolutely necessary.

Reading Part 4

Read the article and answer the questions. **Write a maximum of five words for each answer**. An example is done for you.

Band Hero

What is the hottest thing in music right now? A pair of video games: Guitar Hero Live and Top Band. Anyone can play. The games allow you to become a member of the band. Each game offers a range of pop music hits on game controllers that look and feel like guitars and drums. What makes these video games so much more impressive than "air guitar" is that through the use of something called the Instrument Game Controller the player actually experiences the visceral feeling of performing music. You can even improve if you practise.

So, why not Band Hero? What if I could "play" the horn solo in "Till Eulenspiegel's Merry Pranks" on a "controller horn" or the bassoon solo at the opening of "The Rite of Spring" on a "controller bassoon"? What if I could bang out the timpani part in the first movement of Beethoven's Fifth Symphony or the clarinet solo at the beginning of "Rhapsody in Blue"? What if I could stand in front of the entire orchestra and conduct Mahler's Ninth Symphony? The possibilities are astounding.

The period from the early 1700s through the mid 1930s boasted a rich palate for the Western orchestra. From the Baroque composers such as Bach and Vivaldi through to the transformative Beethoven symphonies and onward to the huge works of Mahler and Shostakovich, the orchestra evolved into a massive vehicle for musical expression. This is when big statements were made - statements that impacted the cultural and political dialogues of the West. Unfortunately, this is a claim the orchestral world can no longer make. Competing now with movies, television, the

Internet and popular music, the orchestra no longer has the platform for cultural dialogue that it once held.

But for me, as a composer, the orchestra still holds a sonic power that is hard to beat. One simple reason is that the orchestra has all the best toys. Some of my favourites include the contra-bassoon, standing five feet tall and covered with knobs and gadgets. It howls deep and dark grumbly tones. The French horn is a conch-like curl of silvery metal plumbing that blasts a clear pure tone; and can be like an angel singing above the choir. The glistening sleek trombones with their sliding tubes are the go-to power machines. When they get boisterous they can easily shake the audience to their core. Another reason, for me, is the magic in the synchronicity of the ensemble - the whole orchestra acting together. A hundred instrumentalists can, with exact accuracy, divide a second into 16 micro-parts and play an off-beat note on any one of those 16th notes. In fact, they do this as a matter of course.

Perhaps the most interesting interaction with classical music that I've had was a commission from the Beethoven Festival in Bonn, Germany, to write a new piece for orchestra that referenced Beethoven in some way. It was a challenging request and for a while I wasn't sure how to proceed. In the end, I decided to take one theme from each movement of Beethoven's Seventh Symphony and work with them as if they were my own. The audience at the premiere of "Rewriting Beethoven's Seventh Symphony," was one of the most musically conservative I've ever faced. I fully realised that what I set out to compose was going to be controversial, especially to Beethoven purists. When the music was over, the audience was decidedly mixed. I was booed and I was called a prophet. But this was one of its successes. It engaged a new audience that usually turns off when new music is presented. The piece built a bridge from the new to the old as it drew from a music that the audience revered. At the opposite end, perhaps, could Band Hero be a bridge for those who are versed in video games but barely know that classical music exists? Controller bassoon, anyone?

No. 1 Practice Paper Tests

Example: Who can play Guitar Hero Live and Top Band?

..................................anybody..................................

1. What is impressive about the video games?

....

2. In which period was the Western orchestra developed as a music expression?

....

3. What is the claim the orchestral world can no longer make?

....

4. Which instrument is well-known for its clear and pure tone?

....

5. For what reason does the author consider classical music magical?

....

6. How does the author describe the audience at the premiere of "Rewriting Beethoven's Seventh Symphony"?

....

7. How does the author characterise his own music?

....

8. What positive result could come from a fresh approach?

....

Writing Part 1

You are a school principal and, recently, students at your school complained about the facilities at your school. The students submitted a survey conducted on fellow students into what facilities they would like to be improved. The results of the survey, are as set out below. Study the survey and write a **report** recommending two of the most necessary improvements that must be made.

Write between 150 and 200 words.

Survey results:

* 57% want the library to be re-stocked with new books
* 82% of students want better equipment in the school gym
* 14% would like the school cafeteria to be enlarged with more seating
* 27% would like the school science labs to be modernised with modern equipment
* 22% want the school playing field to have an area designated as a football pitch

No.1 Practice Paper Tests

Writing Part 2

Write a **composition** describing how you think children have changed, compared to previous generations. Refer to changes in attitudes, opinions and interests with regard to fashion, socialising, hobbies etc.

Write between 250 and 300 words.

LanguageCert
Expert C1
Level 2
International ESOL (Listening, Reading, Writing)
Practice Paper Test 3

Listening Test Audio

Candidate's name (block letters please)

Centre no   **Date**

Time allowed:

Listening   about 30 minutes

Reading and Writing   2 hours and 40 minutes

Instructions to Candidates

- An Answer Sheet will be provided.

- All answers must be transferred to the Answer Sheet.

- Please use a softpencil (2B, HB).

Listening Part 1

You will hear six short, unfinished conversations. Choose the **best reply** to continue each conversation. Put a circle round the letter of the **best reply**. Look at the example. You will hear each conversation **twice**.

Example:

Speaker 1: Is this the right size?

Speaker 2: I think it's OK.

Speaker 1: We should have checked the size before we had bought it.

Speaker 2: ....

    a) Why do you ask?

    (b) You are right, but it's too late now.

    c) I've checked the shop.

1. a) I rather doubt that.

    b) He went alone, in the end.

    c) What's wrong with that?

2. a) It couldn't be any worse.

    b) We shouldn't jump to conclusions.

    c) They seem to have.

3. a) It isn't clear what your plan is.

    b) It was fun to make plans with you.

    c) Just to relax for once.

4. a) I have to; no choice really.

    b) You're not really going, are you?

    c) Serves you right.

5. a) Sure; we have plenty of room.
   b) Perhaps you could've come too.
   c) Yes, it is a long time.

6. a) Yes he did. Just a bit late.
   b) He did. But he didn't deserve it.
   c) I don't think I want to.

Listening Part 2

You will hear three conversations. Listen to the conversations and answer the questions. Put a circle round the letter of the correct answer. You will hear each conversation **twice**. Look at the questions for Conversation One.

Conversation 1

1. What time will the man leave?
   a) 9 am
   b) 3 pm
   c) 5 pm

2. The woman and the man
   a) don't see each other often.
   b) are neighbours.
   c) see each other once a week.

Conversation 2

3. Where are the man and woman?
   a) on a bus
   b) at a restaurant
   c) at the beach

4. The man and woman decide
   a) to go home.
   b) to go to the beach.
   c) to go to a restaurant.

Conversation 3

5. The man is late because
   a) he got lost hiking.
   b) he got lost driving.
   c) he decided to go hiking.

6. The woman was
   a) worried.
   b) sick.
   c) lost.

Listening Part 3

Listen to the person talking and complete the information on the notepad. Write **short** answers of one to five words. You will hear the person **twice**. At the end you will have two minutes to read through and check your answers. You have one minute to look at the notepad. The first one is an example.

DO NOT WRITE MORE THAN 5 WORDS FOR EACH QUESTION.

Birthday Parties for Children

Example:
Name of TV presenter: *Ben*

1. When to decorate child's door:
   ....

2. Two things to decorate house with:
   ....

3. Birthday morning, child taken out for:
   ....

4. Child allowed to choose:
   ....

5. Always congratulate child on:
   ....

6. How to start conversation at dinner:
   ....

7. Most suitable time to give the present:
   ....

Listening Part 4

Listen to the conversation and answer the questions. Put a circle round the letter of the correct answer. An example is done for you. You will hear the conversation **twice**.

Example: Where did Meryl Jones first see "Hello Mama!"?
    (a) on Broadway
    b) in a local movie theatre
    c) in Greece

1. With whom did Meryl Jones went to see *Hello Mama* the first time she saw it?
    a) her ten-year old daughter
    b) her husband
    c) the entire cast of the movie

2. After she saw the musical on Broadway, Meryl Jones
    a) sent a thank-you note to the cast.
    b) went to her daughter's birthday party.
    c) worked as a singer singing the songs.

3. *Hello Mama* was filmed
    a) in Greece.
    b) in London.
    c) in London and in Greece.

4. What did Meryl Jones feel about singing the songs?
    a) She enjoyed it.
    b) She disliked it.
    c) She was dissapointed by the number of songs.

5. What did Meryl Jones think about the producers?

   a) They were very generous.

   b) They were hard to please.

   c) They weren't helpful.

6. Did Meryl Jones do all the stunts herself?

   a) Somebody replaced her in some scenes.

   b) She danced and sang the songs herself.

   c) She could only sing but not dance.

7. What song did Meryl Jones have the most difficult time learning?

   a) *My Heart Goes*

   b) all the *'The Rockies'* songs

   c) the song of the introduction

Reading Part 1

Read the following text, then read the five statements. Some of these statements are true according to the text, some of them are false. Write T for True or F for False in the box next to each statement.

Nail Varnish has been around longer than you might imagine, since at least 3,000 BC. Varnish originated at that time in China. The early mixture was a hodgepodge of bees' wax, gelatin, gum Arabic, and egg whites. Gum Arabic is a natural product found in the African tree of the genus Acacia. The  Chinese also added the petals of flowers such as roses and orchids, and alum to their polish. During the same time period, upper class members in Egypt wore nail varnish similar in texture to lacquer paint. The paint signified money and prosperity. I wonder what colour Cleopatra preferred.

During the Chou Dynasty, around 600 BC, the royal colours were metallic gold and silver. So, the varnish colour choice for royalty was the same. It seemed that whatever the Dynasty colour was, that was the colour worn on people's nails of the Chinese upper class. If the lower class attempted to wear nail varnish, they could be punished by death. The varnish at the time was coloured with natural pigments.

Michelle Menard invented the modern nail varnish in the 1920s. Flapper girls and later, Hollywood starlets wore bright red. Pin-up girls such as Lana Turner always had on the requisite red lips and red nails for photo sessions and walks down the red carpet. Varnish is actually similar to car paint. It requires a remover made of acetone.

Colours range from black to green today. The names are just as diverse and often quite exotic - passion peach, ravishing red, and brave blue are just a few examples. Some men, such as Steven Tyler of *Aerosmith*, are known for wearing varnish. He seems to always have a dark colour such as black on his nails. *Sally's* puts out products designed to colour as well as strengthen your nails. Other companies advertise for nail growth. Modern nail varnishes are produced from nitrocellulose dissolved in a solvent. Nitrocellulose is a polymer derived from cellulose that has been treated with sulfuric and nitric acids. In Florida U.S.A, where the sandal is the shoe of choice, Nail varnish runs rampant.

Keeping your varnish in the refrigerator, as my daughter and I do, will keep the solution from getting clumpy and prolong its shelf life. If you can't put in the refrigerator, keep it away from direct heat and sunlight. Prices range from ninety-nine pence to over twenty-five pounds per bottle. Luckily for all nail varnish wearers of today, you no longer have to be a member of royalty to sport your favourite colour. So go ahead, do like Cleopatra and paint your nails.

1. Nail varnish was first used in Africa. ☐
2. Early nail varnish had egg yolks in it. ☐
3. In China, in 600BC, nail varnish was made of non-artificial dyes. ☐
4. Some companies sell strengthening nail varnish. ☐
5. Keeping nail varnish cold helps it last longer. ☐

Reading Part 2

Read the text and fill the gaps with the correct sentences A-H. Write the letter of the missing sentence in the box in the gap. There are two extra sentences you will not need.

Early Perfume

The use of native aromatic herbs and flowers to sweeten the air had been known for a very long time. **1** It was common for people to wear a garland of flowers, to hang fragrant plants indoors and to add aromatic plants to sweet-smelling rushes when they were spread on a floor. (This last probably started as a Norman custom). In the  making of perfumed preparations, plants were usually used as dried flowers, dried leaves, dried and crushed roots, or extracts in water (by maceration or digestion), oils or fats (and later alcohol). An association between pleasant smells and good health was very widespread so there was considerable overlap between perfumery and healing.

From the 9th century, there was great trade between Byzantium and Venice bringing perfumes into Europe. **2** Arabian perfume arts were very highly developed; having learnt much from the Persians, they used ingredients from China, India and Africa, producing perfumes on a large scale. **3** Al-Hawi, a book by Rhazes, who lived in the late 9th or early 10th century, contained a chapter on cosmetics. **4**

Musk and floral perfumes were brought to northwest Europe in the 11th and 12th centuries from Arabia, through trade with the Islamic world and with the returning

Crusaders. **5** ☐ There are records of the Pepperers Guild of London which go back to 1179; their activities include trade in spices, perfume ingredients and dyes. There are records from the reign of Edward I to show that spices and other aromatic exotic materials were traded in England. Use of alcohol in perfumery was known in northwest Europe in the 12th century but was not widespread until later. A variant of distilled alcohol, rather than alcohol mixed with water, was known in France in the 13th century, prepared by using quicklime in the mix to remove much of the water. Alcohol-based perfume was well known in parts of mainland Europe and came into use in England in the 14th century.

A common technique was to extract essential oil into fat and use it like that or then to remove the essential oil from the fat with alcohol. **6** ☐ Beeswax was used as a base instead of fats and oils sometimes. Pot Pourri was originally made and used wet; it started as the residue of the perfume-making process.

A. There was much trade within Arabia, bringing perfumes from Baghdad to Muslim Spain.

B. Those who traded for these were most often also involved in trade for spices and dyestuffs.

C. These countries had been using distillation since before the 9th century.

D. Another was to heat the plant material in water.

E. However, perfume was common there and in many other places where one might not expect this to be true.

F. Perfume bottles were one of the first common uses for glass.

G. It was translated into Latin in France in the late 12th century.

H. The Romans had introduced many species of aromatic plants to the fringes of the Empire where they were still cultivated.

Reading Part 3

Read the four texts below. There are eight questions about the texts. Decide which text (A, B, C or D) tells you the answer to the question. The first one is done for you.

A.

Cold viruses grow mainly in the nose where they multiply in nasal cells and are present in large quantities in the nasal fluid of people with colds. The highest concentration of cold virus in nasal secretions occurs during the first three days of infection. This is when infected persons are most contagious. Cold viruses may at times be present in the droplets that are expelled in coughs and sneezes. Nasal secretions containing cold viruses contaminate the hands of people with colds as a result of nose blowing, covering sneezes, and touching the nose. Also, cold viruses may contaminate objects and surfaces in the environment of a cold sufferer.

B.

Newborn children acquire temporary immunity to cold viruses from their mother. By six months, this immunity has waned, and children are then susceptible to the over 100 cold viruses. Children have close and intimate contact with their parents and other adults and children. Children are particularly at risk for virus infections which affect the lower airway such as pneumonia and bronchiolitis and to middle ear infection (otitis media). Sinus development is incomplete in young children, but they also develop viral and bacterial sinusitis.

C.

Schisandra Herb

This herb is a shrub native to China. Its berries are used in traditional Chinese medicine to promote the production of body fluids and control coughing, to increase the body's resistance to a broad spectrum of adverse biological, chemical and physical effects. Take twice a day when you have a cold for immediate results.

D.

With some illnesses, a child may be ready to go back to school within a day or two. For example, most viruses that cause the common cold are most contagious before symptoms appear. As a cold progresses, less of the virus is shed through mucus and the child becomes less contagious. However, young children can have quite poor hygiene. If a child is going to cough or sneeze all over classmates, delaying school attendance for a few days should be considered.

In which text does the writer

Example: argue that parents may want to keep their sick child home from school? [D]

1. argue for the benefits of a medicine? □

2. explain how colds are spread? □

3. explain why newborns do not get colds? □

Which text is saying the following?

4. Children aren't always very clean. □

5. If you consume this, you'll feel better right away. □

6. The virus grows in a specific place. □

7. There are quite a few types of cold viruses. □

Reading Part 4

Read the article and answer the questions. **Write a maximum of five words for each answer**. An example is done for you.

William Shakespeare (baptised 26th April 1564 – died 23rd April 1616) was an English poet and playwright, widely regarded as the greatest writer in the English language and the world's preeminent dramatist. He is often referred to as England's national poet and the "Bard of Avon" (or simply "The Bard"). His surviving works consist of 38 plays, 154 sonnets, two long narrative poems, and several other poems. His plays have been translated into every major living language, and are performed more often than those of any other playwright.

Shakespeare was born and raised in Stratford-upon-Avon. At the age of 18 he married Anne Hathaway, who bore him three children: Susanna, and twins Hamnet and Judith. Between 1585 and 1592 he began a successful career in London as an actor, writer, and part owner of the playing company, *The Lord Chamberlain's Men*, later known as the *King's Men*. He appears to have retired to Stratford around 1613, where he died three years later. Few records of Shakespeare's private life survive, and there has been considerable speculation about such matters as his sexuality, religious beliefs, and whether the works attributed to him were written by others.

Shakespeare produced most of his known work between 1590 and 1613. His early plays were mainly comedies and histories, genres he raised to the peak of sophistication and artistry by the end of the sixteenth century. Next he wrote mainly tragedies until about 1608, including *Hamlet, King Lear* and *Macbeth*, which are considered some of the finest examples in the English language. In his last phase, he wrote tragicomedies, also known as romances, and collaborated with other playwrights. Many of his plays were published in editions of varying quality and accuracy during his lifetime, and in 1623 two of his former theatrical colleagues published the *First Folio*, a collected edition of his dramatic works that included all but two of the plays now recognised as Shakespeare's.

Shakespeare was a respected poet and playwright in his own day, but his reputation did not rise to its present heights until the nineteenth century. The Romantics and the Victorians admired him. The Romantics, in particular, acclaimed Shakespeare's genius, and the Victorians hero-worshipped Shakespeare with a reverence that George Bernard Shaw called "bardolatry". In the twentieth century, his work was repeatedly adopted and rediscovered by new movements in scholarship and performance. His plays remain highly popular today and are consistently performed and reinterpreted in diverse cultural and political contexts throughout the world.

Between the Restoration of the monarchy in 1660 and the end of the seventeenth century, classical ideas were in vogue. As a result, critics of the time mostly rated Shakespeare below John Fletcher and Ben Jonson. Thomas Rymer, for example, condemned Shakespeare for mixing the comic with the tragic. Nevertheless, poet and critic John Dryden rated Shakespeare highly, saying of Jonson, "I admire him, but I love Shakespeare". For several decades, Rymer's view held sway; but during the eighteenth century, critics began to respond to Shakespeare on his own terms and acclaim what they termed his natural genius. A series of scholarly editions of his work, notably those of Samuel Johnson in 1765 and Edmond Malone in 1790, added to his growing reputation. By 1800, he was firmly enshrined as the national poet. In the eighteenth and nineteenth centuries, his reputation also spread abroad. Among those who championed him were the writers Voltaire, Goethe, Stendhal and Victor Hugo.

The modernist revolution in the arts during the early twentieth century, far from discarding Shakespeare, eagerly enlisted his work in the service of the Avant

Garde. The *Expressionists* in Germany and the *Futurists* in Moscow mounted productions of his plays. Marxist playwright and director Bertolt Brecht devised an epic theatre under the influence of Shakespeare. The poet and critic T. S. Eliot argued against Shaw that Shakespeare's "primitiveness" in fact made him truly modern. Eliot, along with G. Wilson Knight and the school of New Criticism, led a movement towards a closer reading of Shakespeare's imagery. In the 1950s, a wave of new critical approaches replaced modernism and paved the way for "post-modern" studies of Shakespeare. By the eighties, Shakespeare studies were open to movements such as Structuralism, Feminism and African-American studies.

No.1 Practice Paper Tests

Example: How old was Shakespeare when he got married?

................................eighteen years old................................

1. Where did Shakespeare start his career?

....

2. Why is the legitimacy of the plays still unknown?

....

3. How did Shakespeare's work become renowned even after his death?

....

4. What does the author suggest benefitted his work in recent centuries?

....

5. What kind of diversity characterises Shakespeare's works?

....

6. Why did Thomas Rymer condemn Shakespeare?

....

7. Why did critics disregard the quality of Shakespeare's work?

....

8. What makes Shakespeare so modern according to George Bernard Shaw and T. S. Eliot?

....

Writing Part 1

You have been asked to write a **report** for an environmental group in order to heighten public awareness about the impact of individual households on global warming. Look at the pie chart below and base your report on the findings of the survey and write what recommendations you would make to the public in order to reduce global warming.

Write between 150 and 200 words.

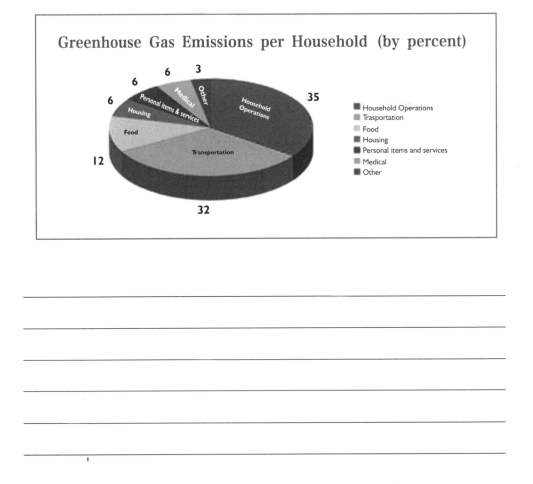

No.1 Practice Paper Tests

Writing Part 2

A friend of yours owns a foreign school and is interested in starting an exchange programme with a school in the UK. He would like, however, to find out more about your hometown, from a resident's point of view. Write an **email** to your friend, detailing the tourist attractions in your city, including cultural and historical sites, in addition to other facilities such as shops, museums, bars etc.

Write between 250 and 300 words.

LanguageCert
Expert C1
Level 2
International ESOL (Listening, Reading, Writing)
Practice Paper Test 4

Listening Test Audio

Candidate's name (block letters please)

Centre no   Date

Time allowed:

Listening   about 30 minutes

Reading and Writing   2 hours and 40 minutes

Instructions to Candidates

- An Answer Sheet will be provided.

- All answers must be transferred to the Answer Sheet.

- Please use a softpencil (2B, HB).

Succeed in LanguageCert Expert CEFR Level C1 ESOL/SELT 朗思全真模拟题

Listening Part 1

You will hear six short, unfinished conversations. Choose the **best reply** to continue each conversation. Put a circle round the letter of the **best reply**. Look at the example. You will hear each conversation **twice**.

Example:

Example:

Speaker 1: Is this the right size?

Speaker 2: I think it's OK.

Speaker 1: We should have checked the size before we had bought it.

Speaker 2: ....

   a) Why do you ask?

   (b) You are right, but it's too late now.

   c) I've checked the shop.

1. a) About what? Can't you tell me?

   b) Why? Am I deaf ?

   c) I can't hear very well any more.

2. a) I thought I didn't make it.

   b) Sometimes I am.

   c) I wouldn't miss it.

3. a) At least 10 times in each room.

   b) Just a few. The room is small.

   c) There's plenty of room for us.

4. a) I'm aware of it.

   b) Don't try so hard.

   c) I'm considering it, though.

5. a) That's nice of you to say.

   b) Excuse me! What did you say you think?

   c) I thought so, but don't take my word for it.

6. a) Recently, I'm told.

   b) Quite far away.

   c) In two days, the latest.

Listening Part 2

You will hear three conversations. Listen to the conversations and answer the questions. Put a circle round the letter of the correct answer. You will hear each conversation **twice**. Look at the questions for Conversation One.

Conversation 1

1. The woman is a
    a) helpful friend.
    b) ferry operator.
    c) travel agent.

2. The man
    a) chooses the first ferry the woman suggests.
    b) isn't as flexible as he thinks.
    c) won't take an overnight ferry.

Conversation 2

3. Where are the man and woman?
    a) in a pub
    b) at a hotel restaurant
    c) at home

4. The man orders
    a) steak.
    b) lobster.
    c) scallops.

Conversation 3

5. Where does this conversation take place?

   a) at a sporting goods store

   b) at a campsite

   c) in a grocery store

6. The man decides

   a) to buy two tents.

   b) to buy a very tall tent.

   c) not to buy a tent at all.

Listening Part 3

Listen to the person talking and complete the information on the notepad. Write **short** answers of one to five words. You will hear the person **twice**. At the end you will have two minutes to read through and check your answers. You have one minute to look at the notepad. The first one is an example.

DO NOT WRITE MORE THAN 5 WORDS FOR EACH QUESTION.

The Great Outdoors

Example:
Illness caused by bad camping equipment: *pneumonia*

1. Name of product advertised:
   ....
2. Type of tent:
   ....
3. Weight:
   ....
4. More space than the:
   ....
5. Lowest temperature window is tested for:
   ....
6. Ideal extra component:
   ....
7. Where you can buy the tent:

No.1　Practice Paper Tests

Listening Part 4

Listen to the conversation and answer the questions. Put a circle round the letter of the correct answer. An example is done for you. You will hear the conversation **twice**.

Example: Which of these things is not mentioned about Jeff Galloway?
   (a) He does television reporting.
   b) He was an Olympic athlete.
   c) He's written books.

1. What race did Mr. Galloway run in the Olympics?
   a) 10 thousand metres
   b) 5 thousand metres
   c) 13 thousand metres

2. As a 13-year-old boy Mr. Galloway was
   a) not sociable.
   b) very good at sports.
   c) sociable and handsome.

3. How did Mr. Galloway begin running?
   a) He wanted to lose weight.
   b) He was forced to by his parents.
   c) He joined a track time and liked it.

4. What is Mr. Galloway's method to teach people to run?
   a) run quickly without breaks
   b) run and then walk and then run again
   c) only walk at first, do not run

5. What is the "magic mile"?

   a) a method of running a mile at a slow pace

   b) running a mile with a lot of breaks

   c) running a mile at a fast pace

6. Who does Mr. Galloway think running is good for?

   a) anyone

   b) adults only

   c) young people

7. Mr. Galloway mentions our ancestors because

   a) they had great endurance.

   b) they ran in competitions.

   c) they had good transportation systems

Reading Part 1

Read the following text, then read the five statements. Some of these statements are true according to the text, some of them are false. Write T for True or F for False in the box next to each statement.

The snow leopard (Uncia uncia), sometimes known as the ounce, is a large cat native to the mountain ranges of Central Asia from Afghanistan, northern Pakistan, to Lake Baikal and eastern Tibet. The taxonomic position of this species has been subject to change. In  the past, many taxonomists included the snow leopard in the genus Panthera, with several of the other largest felids, but later it was placed in its own genus, Uncia. The snow leopard cannot roar, despite possessing an incomplete ossification of the hyoid bone, which was thought to be essential in allowing the big cats to roar. However, new studies show that the ability to roar is due to other morphological features, especially of the larynx, which are absent in the snow leopard. Well known for its beautiful fur, the snow leopard has a whitish-tan coat with ringed spots of dark, ashy-brown and rosettes of black. Its tail is heavy with fur and the bottom of its paws are covered with fur for protection against snow and cold. The life span of a snow leopard is normally 15-18 years, but in captivity it can live up to 20 years.

Weighing usually 35 kilograms (77 lb) to 55 kilograms (121 lb), the snow leopard is slightly smaller on average than a leopard. Exceptionally large males can weigh up to 75 kilograms (165 lb), very small females weigh only 25 kilograms (55 lb). The head and body length is 39-51 in (99-130 cm), the shoulder height is about 24 in (60 cm). The tail measures 32-39 in (81-99 cm) and is proportionately longer than in any other cat species of comparable size. It helps to maintain its balance on the rugged terrain and unstable surfaces of its habitat and is used to cover its nose and mouth in very cold conditions. The head of the snow leopard is relatively small, however the male's head is usually much squarer and wider than that of the female. The big furry feet act as snowshoes, like those of the lynxes.

1. The snow leopard is now part of the "panthera" genus. ☐
2. The snow leopard cannot roar due to an incomplete ossification of the hyoid bone. ☐
3. The snow leopard has a different larynx compared to other similar species. ☐
4. Snow leopards have long tails to keep them balanced. ☐
5. Male snow leopards have wider heads than the female ones. ☐

Reading Part 2

Read the text and fill the gaps with the correct sentences A-H. Write the letter of the missing sentence in the box in the gap. There are two extra sentences you will not need.

Vivienne Westwood

Westwood was born Vivienne Isabel Swire in the village of Tintwistle, Cheshire on April 8 1941, daughter of Dora and Gordon Swire, a storekeeper. **1**____ Vivienne went on to attend Trent Park College and later taught at a primary school in North London.

Vivienne's first husband was Derek Westwood, with whom she had one child, Ben. **2**____ She then met Malcolm McLaren, later known for being the manager for punk bands. The two lived in a council flat in Clapham and had a son named Joseph. **3**____ She still owns the shop, which is at 430 King's Road, and sells her *Anglomania* label from there. The shop is now known as *World's End*.

Together, Westwood and McLaren worked to revolutionise fashion, and the impact is still felt today. **4**____ Her latest collection was about 'gold and treasure, adventure and exploration'. Other influences in Westwood's work have included ethnic Peruvian influence, feminine figure, velvet and knitwear. **5**____

6____ In September 2005, Westwood joined forces with the British civil rights group *Liberty* and launched exclusive limited design T-shirts and baby wear bearing the slogan "I AM NOT A TERRORIST, please don't arrest me". On Easter Sunday 2008, she campaigned in person at the biggest Campaign for Nuclear Disarmament demonstration in ten years, at the Atomic Weapons Establishment, Aldermaston in Berkshire, UK.

A. Their marriage lasted three years.

B. Most notably, she employed the services of Patrick Cox to design shoes for her Clint Eastwood collection in 1984.

C. She attended Glossop Grammar School and studied at the Harrow School of Art for one term.

D. Westwood worked historical factors into her collection by using 17th - 18th century original cutting principles and modernising them.

E. As a teenager in the 1950s, she customised her school uniform to emulate the fashionable pencil skirt.

F. Westwood is also widely known as a political activist.

G. A historical influence has always shown in her work.

H. Westwood continued to teach until 1971, when Malcolm decided to open a shop where Westwood began to sell her outrageous designs.

No.1 Practice Paper Tests

Reading Part 3

Read the four texts below. There are eight questions about the texts. Decide which text (A, B, C or D) tells you the answer to the question. The first one is done for you.

A.

Chocolate comprises a number of raw and processed foods that are produced from the seed of the tropical cacao tree. Native to lowland, tropical South America, cacao has been cultivated for at least three millennia in Central America and Mexico, with its earliest documented use around 1100 BC. The majority of the Mesoamerican peoples made chocolate beverages, including the Maya and Aztecs.

B.

Cacao trees are small, understory trees that need rich, welldrained soils. They naturally grow within 20 degrees of either side of the equator because they need about 2000 millimetres of rainfall a year, and temperatures in the range of 21 to 32 degrees Celsius. Cacao trees cannot tolerate a temperature lower than 15 degrees Celsius (59 degrees Fahrenheit).

The three main varieties of cacao beans used in chocolate are criollo, forastero and trinitario. Representing only five percent of all cacao beans grown, criollo is the rarest and most expensive cacao on the market and is native to Central America, the Caribbean islands and the northern tier of South American states.

C.

The major concern that nutritionists have is that even though eating dark chocolate may favourably affect certain biomarkers of cardiovascular disease, the amount needed to have this effect would provide a relatively large quantity of calories, which, if unused, would promote weight gain.  Obesity is a significant risk factor for many diseases, including cardiovascular disease. As a consequence, consuming large quantities of dark chocolate in an attempt to protect against cardiovascular disease has been described as "cutting off one's nose to spite one's face".

D.

Welcome! to the Coquitlam, Port Moody, Port Coquitlam area of beautiful southwest British Columbia… where culture meets nature, and chocolate is magic! No ordinary chocolate event; our festival inspires, informs, surprises, entertains, and above all celebrates chocolate. Events can be savoured individually, or experienced successively for the ultimate  chocolate experience; the indulgent little escape we all need once in a while. And as if that's not enough, your mere presence grows our mission: mentoring youth in event production and marketing, showcasing emerging artists and performers, and modelling our mindfully appreciative approach to chocolate and to life.

In which text does the writer

Example: invite people to attend an event? | D |

1. refer to ancient people? | |
2. discuss the balance between a health risk and a health benefit? | |
3. discuss types of chocolate beans? | |

Which text is saying the following?

4. Sometimes an indulgence is needed. | |
5. You must be careful not to overindulge while trying to be healthy. | |
6. A degree of heat is need for cacao trees. | |
7. Chocolate was consumed long ago. | |

Reading Part 4

Read the article and answer the questions. **Write a maximum of five words for each answer**. An example is done for you.

Federalists in America

Before the Revolutionary War, the colonies functioned as 13 different and independent governments. Eventually, the Articles of Confederation were adopted to unify the colonies, but when the war ended they were no longer needed. Though a strong central government  was often looked upon by colonists as a threat, delegates were chosen to attend a Constitutional Convention to remake the Articles of Confederation into a centralised constitution. Federalists and Anti-Federalists battled it out either for support of a united country by a federal government or to maintain the status-quo.

The Federalists were primarily lawyers, merchants, planters, and other wealthy citizens. John Jay, James Madison, and Alexander Hamilton wrote some of the more fundamental Federalist papers intended to convince the citizens of New York of the need for a unified central government and to ease their fears of centralised power.

In Federalist Paper two, John Jay claims that the union of America is a logical choice. He cites that Americans are similar: they generally share the same language, religions, and principles of government. He also says that it makes sense to become a whole and cohesive union because the colonies are so near each other. He says, "To all general purposes we have uniformly been one people; each individual citizen everywhere enjoying the same national rights, privileges and protection." He claims that citizens of the colonies had been acting a long time as one, and it was simply time to develop into one veritable country. "By a faction," says James Madison in Federalist ten, "I understand a number of citizens, whether amounting to a majority or minority of the whole, who are united and actuated by some common impulse of passion, or of interest, adverse to the rights of other citizens, or to the permanent and aggregate interests of the community."

Madison deals with the issue of factions and the threat they pose to a united society. He says that human nature makes factions unavoidable and comes to the conclusion that without impeding on one's liberties the only solution to the problem of factions is to control the effects. This is done by having so many factions a majority faction is impossible to achieve. If a faction consists of less than a majority, relief is supplied by the republican principle in that the majority can vote and remove the faction. The federal government is set up in a way which encourages factions. The national government deals with national issues, state governments deal with different state issues, house members have different goals from senate members, the south wants something different from the north, corn farmers want something different from cotton farmers. And everyone has different needs and different wants. The government's job becomes that of regulating factions.

Madison addresses the issue of property rights saying, "Protection of these faculties is the first object of government." And he adds "the most common and curable source of factions had been the various and unequal distribution of property". He foresaw economic factions as important in that they would be inevitably diverse.

Madison talks of separate and distinct parts of government with their own will and independent of other parts of government in Federalist 51. He says a constitution must enable the government to not only control the governed, but also control itself. With a separation of powers, different parts of government control each other and themselves. He feels it is better to have more social problems and less government oppression. The government must be designed for the worst case scenarios of human nature and those who unabashedly seek power. "If men were angels, no government would be necessary. If angels were to govern men, neither external nor internal controls on government would be necessary." he said.

Madison explains that the new constitution and new system for government is handled in a way that separates powers and creates a society and a government broken into so many parts that the rights of individuals and minorities are in little danger from the majority and from those who unjustly seek power.

No.1 Practice Paper Tests

Example: How did the colonies in America worked before the Revolutionary War?

................as different and independent governments...

1. Why was there a sudden change in how the country was governed?

....

2. Why were Federalist papers written?

....

3. How does John Jay view the unity of America?

....

4. What could pose a threat to the Federalists?

....

5. What proposal did Madison make about factions?

....

6. What does Madison feel is important?

....

7. Why does Madison suggest a constitution?

....

8. How does Madison believe the separation of government powers will favour the citizens?

....

Writing Part 1

As a spokesperson for children's charity 'Young Lives Count', you are concerned about the effects of exam anxiety on children's welfare. Below are the results of a recent Childline National Exam Stress Survey. Write an **article** that will be published in a national school newsletter explaining the findings of the survey.

Write between 150 and 200 words.

Childline National Exam Stress Survey conducted on 1300 students:

* 59% of students felt pressure from parents to succeed in exams
* 96% of students felt anxious about exams
* 64% of students reported receiving no support in dealing with exams
* 50% of students have skipped meals due to exam stress
* 66% of students have had trouble sleeping during exams
* 14% of students drank alcohol to relieve exam-related stress

No.1 Practice Paper Tests

Writing Part 2

You would like to invite your friend's child on an adventure weekend away, but you think the mother won't let him/her because she is overprotective. Write a **letter** to your friend outlining the benefits of a weekend away and assuring her that all necessary safety precautions will be taken.

Write between 250 and 300 words.

No.1 Practice Paper Tests

LanguageCert

Expert C1

Level 2

International ESOL (Listening, Reading, Writing)

Practice Paper Test 5

Listening Test Audio

Candidate's name (block letters please)

Centre no   **Date**

Time allowed:

Listening   about 30 minutes

Reading and Writing   2 hours and 40 minutes

Instructions to Candidates

- An Answer Sheet will be provided.

- All answers must be transferred to the Answer Sheet.

- Please use a softpencil (2B, HB).

Listening Part 1

You will hear six short, unfinished conversations. Choose the **best reply** to continue each conversation. Put a circle round the letter of the **best reply**. Look at the example. You will hear each conversation **twice**.

Example:
Speaker 1: Is this the right size?
Speaker 2: I think it's OK.
Speaker 1: We should have checked the size before we had bought it.
Speaker 2: ....
   a) Why do you ask?
   (b) You are right, but it's too late now.
   c) I've checked the shop.

1. a) I've absolutely no idea.
   b) It isn't an issue lately.
   c) We aren't going around here again.

2. a) It isn't happening any more.
   b) It took a long time.
   c) It was a few weeks ago.

3. a) What are you suggesting?
   b) Thank you, I'm glad.
   c) I do, I must admit.

4. a) That would be perfect, wouldn't it?
   b) I doubt that they're on sale.
   c) I said I don't fancy pepperoni.

5. a) I'm not even sure.

   b) It isn't like I'm trying.

   c) I never told him.

6. a) Better safe than sorry I suppose.

   b) Oh, never mind then.

   c) But that's not where we're going.

Listening Part 2

You will hear three conversations. Listen to the conversations and answer the questions. Put a circle round the letter of the correct answer. You will hear each conversation **twice**. Look at the questions for Conversation One.

Conversation 1

1. What is the man's job?
   a) doctor
   b) student
   c) lecturer

2. The man speaks of elements in order to
   a) explain to the woman what medicine was like in the past.
   b) explain to the woman the basics of Ayurvedic medicine.
   c) help the woman cure a fever.

Conversation 2

3. What is the woman asking for?
   a) support
   b) encouragement
   c) advice

4. The man thinks the woman
   a) should switch back to high heels.
   b) shouldn't wear shoes at all.
   c) should wear the shoes for a while.

Conversation 3

5. The man and woman are having a(n)
   a) welcome home party.
   b) anniversary party.
   c) going away party.

6. The woman can be described as
   a) nervous.
   b) jealous.
   c) frustrated.

Listening Part 3

Listen to the person talking and complete the information on the notepad. Write **short** answers of one to five words. You will hear the person **twice**. At the end you will have two minutes to read through and check your answers. You have one minute to look at the notepad. The first one is an example.

DO NOT WRITE MORE THAN 5 WORDS FOR EACH QUESTION.

A Famous Author

Example:

Name: *Ernest Hemingway*

1. Date of his birth:
   ....
2. City of residence in 1920s:
   ....
3. Expatriate community was known as:
   ....
4. Year he received Pulitzer Prize:
   ....
5. Awarded Nobel Prize in 1954 for:
   ....
6. Important impact on development of:
   ....
7. Reason of death:
   ....

Listening Part 4

Listen to the conversation and answer the questions. Put a circle round the letter of the correct answer. An example is done for you. You will hear the conversation **twice**.

Example: The two speakers seem to
  (a) respect each other.
  b) miss each other.
  c) know each other well.

1. What is John Smith well-known for?
   a) He is a famous filmmaker.
   b) He is a famous musician.
   c) He is a famous actor.

2. The woman has created
   a) Anthology film archives.
   b) a Fine Arts school.
   c) a film bookshop.

3. Why can't the man read the woman's original work?
   a) He doesn't speak English.
   b) He can't read her handwriting.
   c) It has to be translated.

4. The woman is
   a) a filmmaker and poet.
   b) a poet.
   c) a film critic.

5. What does the woman claim her home is?

   a) cinema

   b) culture

   c) New York

6. What does the man think about many of the films made in the 1960s?

   a) They were necessary but not necessarily good art.

   b) They were unnecessary.

   c) They were art's reflection of the times.

7. What was the Essential Film Repertory?

   a) a collection of 330 films

   b) 30 carefully selected films

   c) 330 commercial films

No.1 Practice Paper Tests

Reading Part 1

Read the following text, then read the five statements. Some of these statements are true according to the text, some of them are false. Write T for True or F for False in the box next to each statement.

Dairy farming is a class of agricultural, or an animal husbandry enterprise, for long-term production of milk, which may be either processed on-site or transported to a dairy factory for processing and eventual retail sale. Most dairy farms sell the male calves born by their cows, usually for veal production, or breeding depending on the quality of the Bull calf, rather than raising non-milk-producing stock. Many dairy farms also grow their own feed, typically including corn, alfalfa, and hay. This is fed directly to the cows, or is stored as silage for use during the winter season. Additional dietary supplements are added to the feed to increase quality milk production.

Dairy farming has been part of agriculture for thousands of years, but historically, it was usually done on a small scale on mixed farms. Specialist scale dairy farming is only viable where either a large amount of milk is required for production of more durable dairy products such as cheese, or there is a substantial market of people with cash to buy milk, but no cows of their own.

Centralized dairy farming as we understand it primarily developed around villages and cities, where residents were unable to have cows of their own due to a lack of grazing land. Near the town, farmers could make some extra money on the side by having additional animals and selling the milk in town. The dairy farmers would fill barrels with milk in the morning and bring it to market on a wagon.

Before mechanisation most cows were still milked by hand. The first milking machines were an extension of the traditional milk pail. The early milker device fit on top of a regular milk pail and sat on the floor under the cow. Following each cow being milked, the bucket would be dumped into a holding tank.

This developed into the Surge hanging milker. Prior to milking a cow, a large wide leather strap called a surcingle was put around the cow, across the cow's lower back. The milker device and collection tank hung underneath the cow from the strap. This innovation allowed the cow to move around naturally during the milking process rather than having to stand perfectly still over a bucket on the floor.

The next innovation in automatic milking was the milk pipeline. This uses a permanent milk-return pipe and a second vacuum pipe that encircles the barn or milking parlour above the rows of cows, with quick-seal entry ports above each cow. By eliminating the need for the milk container, the milking device shrank in size and weight to the point where it could hang under the cow, held up only by the sucking force of the milker nipples on the cow's udder. The milk is pulled up into the milk-return pipe by the vacuum system, and then flows by gravity to the milkhouse vacuum-breaker that puts the milk in the storage tank. The pipeline system greatly reduced the physical labour of milking since the farmer no longer needed to carry around huge heavy buckets of milk from each cow.

1. Some dairy farms also grow food for their animals. ☐
2. Traditionally, dairy farming was done on small mixed farms. ☐
3. A surcingle is part of a milking machine. ☐
4. Milk pipelines came before Surge hanging milkers. ☐
5. Pipelines made bigger milking devices necessary. ☐

Reading Part 2

Read the text and fill the gaps with the correct sentences A-H. Write the letter of the missing sentence in the box in the gap. There are two extra sentences you will not need.

Psoriasis

Psoriasis is an inflammatory skin condition. **1** ☐ Between 10% and 30% of people who develop psoriasis get a related form of arthritis called "psoriatic arthritis," which causes inflammation of the joints.

Plaque psoriasis is the most common type of psoriasis. **2** ☐ They both frequently form on the elbows, knees, lower back, and scalp. However, the plaques can occur anywhere on the body.

Regardless of type, psoriasis usually causes discomfort. The skin often itches, and it may crack and bleed. **3** ☐

Psoriasis is a chronic, meaning lifelong, condition because there is currently no cure. People often experience flares and remissions throughout their life. Controlling the signs and symptoms typically requires lifelong therapy.

Treatment depends on the severity and type of psoriasis. **4** ☐ A few develop such severe psoriasis that lesions cover most of the body and hospitalisation is required. These represent the extremes. Most cases of psoriasis fall somewhere in between.

More than 4.5 million adults in the United States have been diagnosed with psoriasis, and approximately 150,000 new cases are diagnosed each year. **5** ☐

Psoriasis occurs about equally in males and females. Recent studies show that there may be an ethnic link. It seems that psoriasis is most common in Caucasians and slightly less common in African Americans. Worldwide, psoriasis is most common in Scandinavia and other parts of northern Europe. It appears to be far less common among Asians and is rare in Native Americans. There also is a genetic component associated with psoriasis. Approximately one-third of people who develop psoriasis have at least one family member with the condition.

Research shows that the signs and symptoms of psoriasis usually appear between 15 and 35 years of age. About 75% develop psoriasis before age 40. **6** ☐ After age 40, a peak onset period occurs between 50 and 60 years of age.

A. About 80% of people who develop psoriasis have plaque psoriasis, which appears as patches of raised, reddish skin covered by silvery-white scale.

B. An estimated 20% have moderate to severe psoriasis.

C. Some psoriasis is so mild that the person is unaware of the condition.

D. However, it is possible to develop the condition at any age.

E. All types of psoriasis, ranging from mild to severe, can affect a person's quality of life. Living with this lifelong condition can be physically and emotionally challenging.

F. One woman described her psoriasis as feeling like "a bad sunburn that won't go away."

G. In severe cases, the itching and discomfort may keep a person awake at night, and the pain can make everyday tasks difficult.

H. There are five types, each with unique signs and symptoms.

Reading Part 3

Read the four texts below. There are eight questions about the texts. Decide which text (A, B, C or D) tells you the answer to the question. The first one is done for you.

A.

Television is one of the most prevalent media influences in kids' lives. According to Kids' Take on Media, a survey conducted last year by the National Teachers' Federation, watching TV is a daily pastime for 75 percent of children, both boys and girls from Grade 3 to Grade 10.

How much impact TV has on children depends on many factors: how much they watch, their age and personality, whether they watch alone or with adults, and whether their parents talk with them about what they see on TV.

To minimise the potential negative effects of TV, it's important to understand what the impact of television can be on children.

B.

Television can affect learning and school performance if it cuts into the time kids need for activities crucial to healthy mental and physical development. Most of children's free time, especially during the early formative years, should be spent in activities such as playing, reading, exploring nature, learning about music or participating in sports.

TV viewing is a sedentary activity, and has been proven to be a significant factor in childhood obesity. According to the Heart and Stroke Foundation almost one in four children, between seven and 12, is obese. Time spent in front of the TV is often at the expense of more active pastimes.

C.

Sesame Street is an educational children's television series for young children, though focusing more exclusively on preschoolers in its later years, and is a pioneer of the contemporary educational television standard, combining both  education and entertainment. Sesame Street is well known for its Muppet characters created by Jim Henson. As of now, 4,160 episodes of the show have been produced in 38 seasons. *Sesame Street* is one of the longest-running television shows in history.

As a result of its positive influence, *Sesame Street* is one of the most highly regarded educational shows for children in the world. No other television series has matched its level of international recognition and success. The original series has been televised in 120 countries, and more than 30 international versions have been produced, not including dubbed versions. The series has received 109 Emmy Awards, more than any other television series. An estimated 77 million Americans have watched the series as children; millions more have watched around the world, as have their parents.

D.

Of course, television, in moderation, can be a good thing: Preschoolers can get help learning the alphabet on public television, grade schoolers can learn about wildlife on nature shows and parents can keep up with current events on the evening news.

No doubt about it - TV can be an excellent educator and entertainer.

In which text does the writer

Example: argue that television can be beneficial to children? ☐ D

1. discuss an educational and entertaining show? ☐
2. argue that watching television could be bad for children? ☐
3. stress parents understand television's effect on children? ☐

Which text is saying the following?

4. This TV programme has an excellent reputation. ☐
5. TV can help children learn. ☐
6. Many problems can stem from television watching. ☐
7. A large percent of children watch TV every day. ☐

Reading Part 4

Read the article and answer the questions. **Write a maximum of five words for each answer**. An example is done for you.

The Royal Observatory

The Royal Observatory, home of Greenwich Mean Time and the Prime Meridian line, is one of the most important historic scientific sites in the world. *The Royal Observatory* is the source of the Prime Meridian of the world, Longitude 0° 0' 0''. It is, by international decree, the official starting

point for each new day, year and millennium (at the stroke of midnight GMT as measured from the Prime Meridian). Visitors to the *Observatory* can stand in both the eastern and western hemispheres simultaneously by placing their feet either side of the Prime Meridian: the centre of world time and space.

The *Observatory* was built to improve navigation at sea and 'find the so-much desired longitude of places' (one's exact position east and west) while at sea and out of sight of land, by astronomical means. This was inseparable from the accurate measurement of time, for which the *Observatory* became generally famous in the 19th century.

What is a meridian? What is the Prime Meridian?
A meridian is an arbitrary north-south line used by an astronomer as a zero point from where to take measurements. By comparing thousands of observations taken from the same meridian it is possible to build up an accurate map of the night sky.

The meridian line in Greenwich represents the Prime Meridian of the world,

Longitude Zero (0° 0' 0"). Every place on the Earth is measured in terms of its angle east or west from this line. To stand astride the line is to have one foot in the eastern and one foot in the western hemisphere of the earth; just as the Equator divides the northern and southern hemispheres.

The Prime Meridian at Greenwich passes through a massive special telescope called a transit circle. The transit circle was built by Sir George Airy, the seventh Astronomer Royal, in 1850. The cross-hairs seen in the eyepiece of this transit circle precisely define Longitude 0° for the world.

The 'universal day' is measured from the Prime Meridian. It is the average of a year's worth of 'natural' days and is a scientific time scale used irrespective of time zones.

Since the late 19th century, the Prime Meridian at Greenwich has served as the co-ordinate base for the calculation of Greenwich Mean Time. Before this, almost every town in the world kept its own local time. The Greenwich Meridian was chosen to be the Prime Meridian of the World in 1884. Forty-one delegates from 25 nations met in Washington DC for the International Meridian Conference. By the end of the conference, Greenwich had won the prize of Longitude 0° by a vote of 22 in favour to 1 against (San Domingo), with two abstentions (France and Brazil). There were two main reasons for the victory:

• the USA had already chosen Greenwich as the basis for its own national time-zone system.

• at the time, 72% of the world's commerce depended on sea-charts which used Greenwich as the Prime Meridian.

The decision, essentially, was based on the argument that by naming Greenwich as Longitude 0°, it would······

Example: How was the Royal Observatory recognised as the starting point for the measurement of time?

..................by international decree...

1. What is so special about being at The Royal Observatory?

   ....

2. What was the initial reason for the building of the Royal Observatory?

   ....

3. What else does the author suggest the meridian line is used for?

   ....

4. What can standing on the meridian line be compared with?

   ....

5. When was the 'transit circle' built?

   ....

6. How did the world benefit from centralising time?

   ....

7. How has the world calculated precise time since the late 19th century?

   ....

8. What does the author suggest was the reason the vote was swayed towards the current location?

   ....

Writing Part 1

As part of National Reading Week, you would like to encourage the students in your class to start reading more. Based on the results of the survey below, of over 8,000 primary and secondary pupils in the U.K, send a **letter** to the pupils' parents, outlining the key problem areas in encouraging children to read and making suggestions as to how to encourage more children to read books.

Write between 150 and 200 words.

Survey findings in children's reading preferences and reading behaviours:
* 40% of children said they enjoy reading
* 50% of the sample believed they didn't read enough
* 86% of children held positive attitudes to reading
* 15% of children only read because they 'have to'
* 83% of the sample appreciate the importance of reading as a life skill
* 78% of pupils said they would read if they had more time
* 81% of the sample stated that they would read more if books were cheaper
* 50% of children believe that websites/celebrity endorsement would encourage them to read more

Writing Part 2

Your English teacher has asked you to write a **composition** about your upbringing, the rules your parents imposed on you and whether you would bring up your child any differently.

Write between 250 and 300 words.

No.2

Speaking Tests ESOL

Test 1

Part 1 (3 minutes)

I: Interlocutor, C: Candidate

I: *(Give today's date.)*

(Give candidate's name.) Test begins. Hello. My name's *(give full name)*. Can you spell your family name for me please?

C: *(Spells family name.)*

I: Thank you. And where are you from?

C: *(Responds.)*

I: Thank you. Now, in the first part of the test I'm going to ask you some questions about yourself and your ideas.

(Choose up to five questions, one from each of the different topic areas, as time allows. Name the topic; eg "Now, Travel".)

Topics

Personal details

- Describe yourself as a person.
- What are your strengths and weaknesses?
- If you could change something on you, what would that be?
- Have you ever wished you were someone else?

Your family

- Describe your family.
- How important do you think family is?
- What are the advantages/disadvantages of living with your family?
- Which family member do you feel more close to?

Cinema

- How often do you go to the cinema? What kind of films are you interested in?
- Do you spend time reading reviews before going to watch a film? Do you trust them?
- What is the best/worst film you have ever seen?
- Who is your favourite actor/actress?

Travel

- Do you like travelling alone or in a group?
- Are you fond of long- or short-distance travelling?
- Name three things that you always take with you when you travel.
- What means of transport do you prefer travelling by?

Arts

- Are you interested in the arts? Which art do you like the most?
- Who is your favourite artist?
- Tell me about a museum/archeological site/gallery you have visited.
- To what extent do you feel that art imitates life?

C: (*Responds.*)

I: (*Makes brief responses and/or comments.*)

I: Thank you.

Part 2 (3 minutes)

I: Now, Part Two. We are going to role-play some situations. I want you to start or respond. First situation (choose one situation from **A**).

A

- We're friends. I start.

  I'm planning a holiday with my family. Any suggestions?

- I'm your dance instructor. I start.

  You are very talented. What are your plans for dancing in the future?

- I'm your neighbour. I start.

  Did you hear that racket last night? What happened?

- We work together. I start.

  I need to take next week off. How should I tell our boss?

C: *(Responds.)*

I: *(Role-play the situation with candidate - approximately two turns each.)*

I: Second situation (choose one situation from **B**).

B

- We're best friends. You want to know what I want for my birthday. You start.

- I'm a relative who doesn't live with you. You want to visit me. You start.

- I'm a friend you met over the Internet. You would like to meet me. You start.

- I'm your new English teacher. You want to know what your class will be like now. You start.

C: *(Initiates.)*

I: *(Role-play the situation with candidate – approximately two turns each.)*

I: *(Role-play a third situation from A or **B if time allows.**)*

I: Thank you.

Part 3 (4 minutes)

I: Now Part Three. In this part of the test we're going to discuss something together. All right?

Here are some qualities a good friend must have. *(Hand over candidate's task sheet.)* Let's discuss what we think about these things and decide which ones we think are the most important.

Take twenty seconds to think about what you want to say. *(Wait 20 seconds.)* Why don't you start?

Interlocutor's Task Sheet & Candidate's Task Sheet

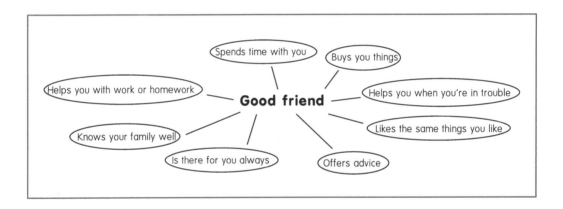

I: Thank you. (Retrieve candidate's task sheet.)

No.2 Speaking Tests ESOL

Part 4 (5 minutes)

I: In Part Four you are going to talk about something for two minutes. Your topic is (choose topic for candidate).

Topics
A   Soft drugs should be legalised.
B   An experience that changed your life.
C   Superstitions are childish.

I: You now have thirty seconds to write some notes to help you. *(Hand over a piece of paper and pen/pencil.)* So your topic is *(repeat topic). (Withdraw eye contact for thirty seconds. Leave recorder running.)*

I: *(Candidate's name)*, please start.

C: *(Talks.)*

I: *(When candidate has talked for a maximum of two minutes, say, 'Thank you', and then ask some follow-up questions.)*

Follow-up questions
Soft drugs should be legalised.
○   What would you do if you learnt that your friend is a drug addict?
○   Should the state impose heavier punishment to drug dealers?
○   How should drug addicts be treated?
○   What do you know about rehabilitation centres in your country?

An experience that changed your life.
○   How important is to learn from experience?
○   Why do people often repeat their mistakes?
○   Should people be discouraged or reluctant to take risks based on previous bad experience?
○   Do you believe that the course of history is circular?

Superstitions are childish.

- Do you believe in the paranormal?
- How would you react if you saw something that looked like a ghost?
- Only ignorant people are superstitious. Do you agree?
- Should scientists keep investigating the paranormal?

I: Thank you. *(Give candidate's name.)* That is the end of the exam.

No.2 Speaking Tests ESOL

Test 2

Part 1 (3 minutes)

I: *Interlocutor*, **C:** *Candidate*

I: (Give today's date.)
(Give candidate's name.) **Test begins.** Hello. My name's (give full name). Can you spell your family name for me please?

C: (Spells family name.)

I: Thank you. And where are you from?

C: (Responds.)

I: Thank you. Now, in the first part of the test I'm going to ask you some questions about yourself and your ideas.

(Choose up to five questions, one from each of the different topic areas, as time allows. Name the topic; eg 'Now, At home'.)

Topics

At home

- Describe the place where you live.
- If you had the chance to change something in your house, what would that be?
- Describe your ideal place of living.
- Which room do you spend most of your time in?

At work

- Have you got a job? If so, what are your duties and responsibilities? If not, what are you currently doing?
- Describe your ideal job.
- What are the main reasons for the increase in unemployment nowadays?
- What should the state do to reduce unemployment?

TV

- How often do you watch TV? What kind of programmes are you interested in?
- Tell me about the best/worst TV programme you have ever watched.
- What do you think of reality shows?
- In your opinion, how much does TV influence the course of our lives?

Holidays

- Describe the best/worst holidays you have ever had.
- Name five things that you always take with you when you go on holidays.
- Do you like visiting the same place twice?
- Do you prefer having a travel agency organizing your holiday or planning it yourself?

The past

- Tell me about a funny/unexpected/fascinating experience you had in the past.
- If you could change something in your past, what would that be?
- How have your past experiences helped you become the person you are today?
- If you could relive one day/moment of your past life, what would that be?

C: *(Responds.)*

I: *(Make brief responses and/or comments.)*

I: Thank you.

No.2 Speaking Tests ESOL

Part 2 (3 minutes)

I: Now, Part Two. We are going to role-play some situations. I want you to start or respond. First situation (choose one situation from **A**).

A

- We're friends. I start.

  I'm going on holiday where you went last year.
  Any suggestions of what to do there?

- I'm your music instructor. I start.

  You are very talented. Do you want to have a solo in the upcoming performance?

- I'm your neighbour. I start.

  I'm selling my apartment. Do you know anyone who may be interested in buying it?

- We work together. I start.

  I have so much to do today! How should I manage my time?

C: *(Responds.)*
I: *(Role-play the situation with candidate - approximately two turns each.)*
I: *Second situation (choose one situation from **B**).*

B

- I'm your friend. You want to know if I want to get dinner with you. You start.

- I'm a relative. You want to help planning a family party. You start.

- I'm a friend. You want to borrow something from me. You start.

- I'm your new teacher. You want to know if you'll have a lot of homework this year. You start.

C: *(Initiates.)*

I: *(Role-play the situation with candidate - approximately two turns each.)*

I: *(Role-play a third situation from **A** or **B if time allows**.)*

I: *Thank you.*

No.2 Speaking Tests ESOL

Part 3 (4 minutes)

I: Now Part Three. In this part of the test we're going to discuss something together. All right?

We've been asked to rank a list of ways to get healthier. Let's discuss these ideas and try to agree on their order of effectiveness. *(Hand over candidate's task sheet.)*

Take twenty seconds to think about what you want to say. *(Wait 20 seconds.)* Why don't you start?

Interlocutor's Task Sheet & Candidate's Task Sheet

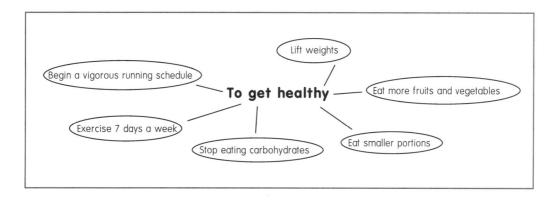

I: Thank you. (Retrieve candidate's task sheet.)

Part 4 (5 minutes)

I: In Part Four you are going to talk about something for two minutes. Your topic is (choose topic for candidate).

Topics

A Divorce rates are increasing over the years.

B A celebrity you would like to meet.

C Punishment should fit the crime.

I: You now have thirty seconds to write some notes to help you. *(Hand over a piece of paper and pen/pencil.)* So your topic is *(repeat topic). (Withdraw eye contact for thirty seconds. Leave recorder running.)*

I: *(Candidate's name)*, please start.

C: *(Talks.)*

I: *(When candidate has talked for a maximum of two minutes, say, 'Thank you', and then ask some follow-up questions.)*

Follow-up questions

Divorce rates are increasing over the years.

○ What makes human relationships so fragile nowadays?

○ What should people do to protect their relationship?

○ Should 'free-cohabitation' be legalised?

○ What do you think are some of the pros and cons of 'free-cohabitation'?

A celebrity you would like to meet.

○ What are some of the questions that you would like to ask him/her?

○ What problems do you imagine this person faces?

○ What would you do if you were in his/her shoes for one day?

○ Why do young people desire fame?

No.2 Speaking Tests ESOL

> **Punishment should fit the crime.**
> - Death penalty should return for some crimes, do you agree?
> - Is life imprisonment a fair punishment for a drug dealer or a serial killer?
> - Do you believe that the legal system in your country should be revised? In what ways?
> - How do you feel about the rights of the guilty? Should correctional facilities be improved to offer better living conditions to the prisoners?

I: Thank you. *(Give candidate's name.)* That is the end of the exam.

Test 3

Part 1 (3 minutes)

I: *Interlocutor*, **C:** *Candidate*

I: (Give today's date.)

(Give candidate's name.) Test begins. Hello. My name's (give full name). Can you spell your family name for me please?

C: (Spells family name.)

I: Thank you. And where are you from?

C: (Responds.)

I: Thank you. Now, in the first part of the test I'm going to ask you some questions about yourself and your ideas.

(Choose up to five questions, one from each of the different topic areas, as time allows. Name the topic; eg "Education".)

Topics

Education

- How far have you gone or do you wish to go with your education?
- What is/was your best/worst subject in school?
- Who is/was your favourite teacher?
- How important do you think education is?

Sports

- What kind of sports are you interested in?
- If you were given the chance to take up a new sport, what would that be?
- What qualities one should possess in order to join a team sport?
- 'A healthy mind lies in a healthy body'. Do you agree?

Reading

- How much time do you spend on reading (excluding your homework)? What kind of books are you interested in?
- Tell me about the best/worst book you have ever read.
- Who is your favourite writer/author?
- In what ways can reading help a person grow?

Fashion

- How much money do you spend on clothes?
- How closely do you follow fashion trends?
- Would you buy something just because it has a designer signature?
- How often do you buy new clothes? Do you throw away your old clothes when fashion changes?

The future

- What are your aspirations for the future?
- How do you imagine yourself in ten years' time?
- Would you be interested in knowing your own future?
- Would you prefer to live in the future or the past?

C: *(Responds.)*

I: (Make brief responses and/or comments.)

I: Thank you.

Part 2 (3 minutes)

I: Now, Part Two. We are going to role-play some situations. I want you to start or respond. First situation (choose one situation from **A**).

A

- We're friends. I start.

    I'm going to take a friend out to dinner.
    Can you suggest where we should go?

- I'm the director in a theatre production you're in. I start.

    You are very talented. Do you hope to continue acting?

- I'm your neighbour. I start.

    I found a box of things on the stairs. Is it yours?

- We work together. I start.

    You are thinking of quitting? But why do you want to stop working here?

C: *(Responds.)*

I: *(Role-play the situation with candidate - approximately two turns each.)*

I: Second situation *(choose one situation from **B**).*

B

- We're friends. You want to go shopping with me tomorrow. You start.

- We're relatives. You want to know what I want for my birthday. You start.

- We're siblings. You want to know if you can borrow something from me. You start.

- I'm a salesperson. You want to know what to buy as a wedding present for a friend. You start.

C: *(Initiates.)*

I: *(Role-play the situation with candidate - approximately two turns each.)*

I: *(Role-play a third situation from A or **B if time allows**.)*

I: Thank you.

Part 3 (4 minutes)

I: Now Part Three. In this part of the test we're going to discuss something together. All right?

Here are some quotations about global warming. *(Hand over candidate's task sheet.)*

Let's discuss the quotations and decide which ones we most agree with and which ones we least agree with.

Take twenty seconds to think about what you want to say. *(Wait 20 seconds.)* Why don't you start?

Interlocutor's Task Sheet & Candidate's Task Sheet

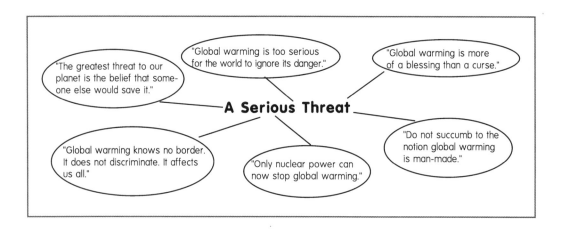

I: Thank you. (Retrieve candidate's task sheet.)

Part 4 (5 minutes)

I: In Part Four you are going to talk about something for two minutes. Your topic is *(choose topic for candidate)*.

Topics
A The freedom of the press.
B A bad job is better than unemployment.
C Money makes the world go round.

I: You now have thirty seconds to write some notes to help you. *(Hand over piece of paper and pen/pencil.)* So your topic is *(repeat topic)*. *(Withdraw eye contact for thirty seconds. Leave recorder running.)*

I: *(Candidate's name)*, please start.

C: *(Talks.)*

I: *(When candidate has talked for a maximum of two minutes, say, 'Thank you', and then ask some follow-up questions.)*

Follow-up questions
The freedom of the press
○ How important is to be well informed about national and international events?
○ Can a newspaper truly be objective?
○ How should people choose which newspaper to read?
○ Should there be an organisation to control the freedom of the press?

A bad job is better than unemployment.
○ What factors should influence our choosing or staying in a job?
○ What should the state do to protect employees and ensure better working conditions?
○ What qualities an employer should possess?
○ Do you think there will be more work opportunities in the future?

Money makes the world go round.
- Money can't buy happiness. Do you agree?
- Is it a good idea to save as much money as you can?
- What problems do you imagine a millionaire faces?
- Money or Fame? What do you think is more important?

I: Thank you. *(Give candidate's name.)* That is the end of the exam.

No.2 Speaking Tests ESOL

Test 4

Part 1 (3 minutes)

I: *Interlocutor*, **C:** *Candidate*

I: (Give today's date.)

(Give candidate's name.) **Test begins. Hello. My name's** (give full name). **Can you spell your family name for me please?**

C: (Spells family name.)

I: Thank you. And where are you from?

C: (Responds.)

I: Thank you. Now, in the first part of the test I'm going to ask you some questions about yourself and your ideas.

(Choose up to five questions, one from each of the different topic areas, as time allows. Name the topic; eg 'Now, Free time'.)

Topics

Free time

- How much free time do you have?
- How do you choose to spend your free time?
- What is your favourite past-time activity?
- How important do you think free time is?

Theatre

- How often do you go to the theatre? What kind of plays are you interested in?
- Have you ever watched ancient theatre? How do you feel about it?
- Tell me about the best/worst play you have ever seen.
- How do you choose what play you are going to see?
  What makes a good play?

Technology
- In your opinion, how has technology made our lives better?
- What is the best/worst technological invention?
- Name some of the threats that technology poses to people nowadays.
- What steps of action should be taken in order to keep the increased use of technology under control?

Space
- Would you be interested in travelling into space?
- How much do you know about space exploration?
- How do you feel about the huge amounts of money spent on space exploration?
- Name some pros and cons of being an astronaut.

Computers/Internet
- Computers have become a necessity nowadays. Do you agree?
- Name some of the advantages and disadvantages of using a computer.
- Do you use the Internet? How often and what for?
- Are you aware of any dangers that using the Internet might hide?

C: *(Responds.)*

I: (Make brief responses and/or comments.)

I: Thank you.

No.2 Speaking Tests ESOL

Part 2 (3 minutes)

I: Now, Part Two. We are going to role-play some situations. I want you to start or respond. First situation (choose one situation from *A*).

A

- We're friends. I start.

  I'm going shopping. Would you like to come with me?

- I'm your English teacher. I start.

  I know you've had a hard time in class this year. Have things been any better lately?

- I'm your neighbour. I start.

  I heard about a concert by the river tonight.
  Do you want to go with me?

- We work together. I start.

  You are very busy. Do you want some help with all that work?

C: *(Responds.)*
I: *(Role-play the situation with candidate - approximately two turns each.)*
I: *Second situation (choose one situation from **B**).*

B

- We're friends. You want to borrow something from me. You start.

- I work at a hardware store. You want to buy paint to paint your bedroom. You start.

- I'm your dance instructor. You want to know if I think you're a good student. You start.

- I work in a shoe store. You don't know what to buy. You start.

C: *(Initiates.)*
I: *(Role-play the situation with candidate - approximately two turns each.)*
I: *(Role-play a third situation from A or **B if time allows**.)*
I: Thank you.

Part 3 (4 minutes)

I: Now Part Three. In this part of the test we're going to discuss something together. All right?

Here is a list of some things people like doing in their free time. *(Hand over candidate's task sheet.)* Let's discuss both their positive and negative aspects and then decide which one is the most, and which the least, beneficial for people.

Take twenty seconds to think about what you want to say. *(Wait 20 seconds.)* Why don't you start?

Interlocutor's Task Sheet & Candidate's Task Sheet

I: Thank you. (Retrieve candidate's task sheet.)

Part 4 (5 minutes)

I: In Part Four you are going to talk about something for two minutes. Your topic is (choose topic for candidate)

Topics
A Silence is gold.
B Means of transport.
C The importance of welfare organisations.

I: You now have thirty seconds to write some notes to help you. *(Hand over piece of paper and pen/pencil.)* So your topic is *(repeat topic). (Withdraw eye contact for thirty seconds. Leave recorder running.)*

I: *(Candidate's name)*, please start.

C: *(Talks.)*

I: *(When candidate has talked for a maximum of two minutes, say, 'Thank you', and then ask some follow-up questions.)*

Follow-up questions

Silence is gold.
- Are there cases where silence might not be a good thing?
- What if by voicing an argument you hurt or provoke somebody's feelings?
- Not telling the truth is not the same as telling a lie, do you agree?
- You must always speak up for yourself no matter what, do you agree?

Means of transport.
- Do people nowadays feel safe when using public transportation?
- Airplane is considered to be the safest means of transport, do you agree?
- What steps of action should be taken to reduce traffic jam especially in the city centre?
- What should the state do to improve quality of transport services?

The importance of welfare organisations.
- Why should anyone give his/her time or money to charity?
- Are you aware of any welfare organisations operating in your country?
- What should the state do to help welfare organisations in their work?
- How can welfare organisations help people in need?

I: Thank you. *(Give candidate's name.)* That is the end of the exam.

Test 5

Part 1 (3 minutes)

I: *Interlocutor*, **C:** *Candidate*

I: (Give today's date.)

(Give candidate's name.) Test begins. Hello. My name's (give full name). Can you spell your family name for me please?

C: (Spells family name.)

I: Thank you. And where are you from?

C: (Responds.)

I: Thank you. Now, in the first part of the test I'm going to ask you some questions about yourself and your ideas.

(Choose up to five questions, one from each of the different topic areas, as time allows. Name the topic; eg 'Now, Your friends'.)

Topics

Your friends

- Do you have many friends?
- What things do you share with your friends?
- Are you open to making new friends?
- What are the most important qualities a friend should possess?

Music

- What kind of music do you enjoy listening to?
- Who is your favourite musician?
- Have you ever been to a live music concert?
- Do you pay more attention to the music or the lyrics of a song?

Food

- Do you know how to cook? What is your speciality?
- Do you prefer eating in or going out?
- What is your favourite dish/food?
- What do you think of fast food / take-away food?

Environment

- What is the biggest threat of the environment nowadays?
- What should people do to protect the environment?
- Name three steps of action that the state should take for the protection of the environment.
- Heavy fines must be imposed to those polluting the environment, do you agree?

Celebrities

- Who is your favourite celebrity?
- Would you like to be famous? What would you be willing to sacrifice in order to achieve this?
- Name two pros and cons of being famous.
- Why do you think people are so interested in learning as much as they can about the lives of celebrities?

C: (*Responds.*)

I: (*Make brief responses and/or comments.*)

I: Thank you.

Part 2 (3 minutes)

I: Now, Part Two. We are going to role-play some situations. I want you to start or respond. First situation (*choose one situation from* **A**).

A

- We're friends. I start.
  I want to go somewhere fun tonight. Can you suggest any place I should go to?

- I'm an old friend of your family. I start.
  I haven't seen you in ages. Where have you been?

- I'm your neighbour. I start.
  I found a kitten this morning. Would you mind taking care of it for the night?

- We work together. I start.
  I want to take a long holiday. Where are you going to go?

C: (*Responds*.)
I: (*Role-play the situation with candidate - approximately two turns each.*)
I: Second situation (*choose one situation from* **B**).

B

- We're friends. You want me to join your English class. You start.

- I'm a relative. You want to visit me. You start.

- We work together. You want to know if I can cover your shift tomorrow. You start.

- I'm a police officer. You want to know if I've seen your lost dog. You start.

C: (*Initiates*.)
I: (*Role-play the situation with candidate - approximately two turns each.*)
I: (*Role-play a third situation from A or **B if time allows**.*)
I: Thank you.

Part 3 (4 minutes)

I: Now Part Three. In this part of the test we're going to discuss something together. All right?

We've been asked to rank a list of suggestions for holiday destinations. (*Hand over candidate's task sheet.*) Let's discuss these places and try to agree on their order of interest.

Take twenty seconds to think about what you want to say. (*Wait 20 seconds.*) Why don't you start?

Interlocutor's Task Sheet & Candidate's Task Sheet

I: Thank you. (Retrieve candidate's task sheet.)

No.2 Speaking Tests ESOL

Part 4 (5 minutes)

I: In Part Four you are going to talk about something for two minutes. Your topic is (*choose topic for candidate*).

Topics

A **The effects of alcohol.**

B **The importance of a good educational system.**

C **Bullying should be punished.**

I: You now have thirty seconds to write some notes to help you. (*Hand over a piece of paper and pen/pencil.*) So your topic is (*repeat topic*). (*Withdraw eye contact for thirty seconds. Leave recorder running.*)

I: (*Candidate's name*), please start.

C: (*Talks.*)

I: (*When candidate has talked for a maximum of two minutes, say, 'Thank you', and then ask some follow-up questions.*)

Follow-up questions

The effects of alcohol.

○ Do TV commercials encourage people to drink?

○ Advertisements for alcohol should be banned, do you agree?

○ How should an alcoholic be treated?

○ How should children be educated about the dangers of alcohol?

The importance of a good educational system.

○ In your opinion, what are the strengths/weaknesses of the current educational system?

○ The educational system should stay untouched by governments, do you agree?

○ What should the state do to improve the quality of education in your country?

○ Do you think that private universities could harm public education? If so, in what ways?

Bullying should be punished.
- How do you imagine a victim of bullying feels?
- Where can incidents of bullying occur?
- What should the state do to reduce incidents of bullying?
- What is the right course of action that a victim of bullying should adopt?

I: Thank you. (*Give candidate's name.*) That is the end of the exam.

No.3

Audio Scripts

Test 1

Part one, part one

You will hear six short, unfinished conversations. Choose the **best reply** to continue each conversation. Put a circle round the letter of the **best reply**. Look at the example. *(15 seconds)* You will hear each conversation twice.

Number one. Number one. *(6 seconds)*

F: What a beautiful morning!

M: But it might as well not be, since we're stuck inside working.

F: Stop acting like that!

(Wait 10 seconds before repeating.) (10 seconds)

Number two. Number two. *(6 seconds)*

M: Louise! Hi! How are you?

F: Mike! What a surprise; I thought you lived in Fernhill!

M: I do, but I always shop here.

(Wait 10 seconds before repeating.) (10 seconds)

Number three. Number three. *(6 seconds)*

M: You look a bit rough; are you OK?

F: I've got a terrible headache. I've just bought some aspirin.

M: Where are you heading now?

(Wait 10 seconds before repeating.) (10 seconds)

Number four. Number four. *(6 seconds)*

M: Wow, look at that car!

F: Each to his own.

M: What? You don't like it?

(Wait 10 seconds before repeating.) (10 seconds)

Number five. Number five. *(6 seconds)*

F: That girl's always there playing the violin.

M: Well, she's certainly talented.

F: That piece isn't so difficult; I know how to play it.

(Wait 10 seconds before repeating.) (10 seconds)

Number six. Number six. *(6 seconds)*

F: We'll start when Maria gets here.

M: I just saw her in the hall.

F: I wonder where she went.

(Wait 10 seconds before repeating.) (10 seconds)

That is the end of Part One.

Part two, part two

You will hear three conversations, Listen to the conversations and answer the questions. Put a circle round the letter of the correct answer. You will hear each conversation twice. Look at the questions for Conversation One. *(10 seconds)*

Conversation One

M: Brenda? Oh my! Brenda! I can't believe it is really you!

W: Mike! It is so lovely to see your face! How are you? What's going on?

M: I'm fine, doing really well actually. I haven't seen you in ages!

W: Yes, well, actually I've been working in America for the past year. I haven't been back here in 13 months. Can you believe it?

M: I heard you were in America but I didn't realise it had been so long. Are you happy to be back?

W: Yes, of course I am. But, I do miss it there. I made so many wonderful friends and they're so far away now. That's the problem with traveling and living in different places, you're always missing someone or something or some place.

M: I know what you mean. Better to just stay in one place like me!

W: But don't you miss all your friends who have left town?

M: That's true, but at least they always know where to find me!

(Wait 10 seconds before repeating.) (10 seconds)

Now, look at the questions for Conversation Two. (10 seconds)

Conversation Two

W: So are you interested in this internship for my campaign?

M: I think so, but I'd like to know exactly what I'd be doing if I accepted it.

W: Basically you'll be working with me doing event planning. Our next event is at a pub in Manchester. You'd be in charge of finding a band to play and sorting out some other details.

M: Can I get school credit for it?

W: That's really up to your school. I'm perfectly willing to do that.

M: Great, I think I'd like to do it. Let me contact my advisor at school and then I'll get back to you.

W: That sounds great. Just make sure to call me before Friday because I need to get things started by then.

(Wait 10 seconds before repeating.) (10 seconds)

Now, look at the questions for Conversation Three. (10 seconds)

Conversation Three

W: I would like to buy a programme that plays DVDs for my computer.

M: You don't already have one? Most computers come with them.

W: I know, but I really dislike the programme I have. You can't maximise the screen and the controller is difficult to use.

M: I understand, what kind of computer do you have?

W: An Acer 360.

M: I'm not sure what programme comes with that, but I have this programme here for only 20 pounds that will work with your Windows operating system. It is called "My DVD". And, it comes with a FREE remote control. That means you can watch DVDs on your computer without standing up and messing around with the controls.

W: That sounds perfect. I'll take it. Actually, I should just check, do you have anything else cheaper?

M: We have one programme for 15 pounds but it isn't nearly as nice, and that's only a 5 pound difference!

W: Okay, I'll take the first one. *(Wait 10 seconds before repeating.) (10 seconds)*

That is the end of Part Two.

Part three, part three

Listen to the person talking and complete the information on the notepad. Write short answers of one to five words. You will hear the person twice. At the end you will have two minutes to read through and check your answers. You have one minute to look at the notepad. The first one is an example. *(1 minute)*

[beep]

"Processing the Work of The Secret Government" is a thought-provoking documentary that examines American foreign and home policy. Its aim is to open the eyes of the public to the machinations underlying American politics, bringing to light the covert national and international operations the United States government has taken part in. It begins by outlining the Iran-Contra affair. The documentary claims that at the time of the affair, the US was fighting a proxy war with the Soviet Union, by trying to overthrow the Nicaraguan Sandinista government, which the U.S claimed, had communist ties.

When congress wouldn't fund the Contras (the terrorist group the Reagan Administration wanted to train to go into Nicaragua to fight) Reagan took matters into his own hands. A group of companies and private donors was formed, called *'The Enterprise'*. This group was essentially in it for the money, but members were also united in their mission to fund the Contras and overthrow the Nicaraguan government. The group itself was utterly unscrupulous, also making millions on the side by such illegal ventures as selling weapons to Iran while the US was an ally of Iraq, and the two countries were at war. This tangled stated of affairs was complicated all the more by *The Enterprise* also selling marked-up weapons to the Contras, the group they were supposedly helping.

The documentary focuses on the secrecy of the U.S government - and the innate problems that secrecy poses for the American people. It claims the secret government is a law unto itself with no constitution. It also highlights some other secret operations the U.S government had taken part in prior to the Iran-Contra affair. Among others, the overthrow of Guatemala's ruler, Arbenz is mentioned. The documentary claims that the U.S.A had a vested interest in Guatemala at the time, since the US *United Fruit Company,* owned vast swathes of land in the Caribbean and dominated the market in fruit exports, particularly bananas. Hence, according to the documentary, a CIA-backed revolt overthrew the Arbenz government in order to secure the US export of fruit, because Arbenz had wanted land reform. Had Arbenz had his way, *United Fruit* would have lost land to peasants, causing a massive financial loss to the U.S company. Ostensibly, however, the coup was instigated to depose the communist government led by Arbenz, which was in opposition to U.S political interest.

The US invasions of Cuba and assassination attempts on Fidel Castro are also focused on, as well as the fact that Vietnam was initially a covert operation with 1500 people there, labelled 'advisors'. In both cases, again as with Guatemala, the need to stamp out a perceived communist threat was the motivation for invasion. The film also brought up the Watergate scandal in an attempt to highlight yet another example of the 'secret government' that operates behind closed doors and to which the public is all but totally oblivious. In this last case, President Nixon's government is believed to have been behind the attempt to wiretap phones and steal secret documents from the Democratic National Committee. Although Nixon was never prosecuted, the Watergate scandal changed American politics forever, leading many Americans to question their leaders and to think more critically about the presidency.

(Wait 10 seconds before repeating.) (10 seconds)
You will now have two minutes to read through and check your answers. (2 minutes)
[beep]
That is the end of Part Three.

Part four, part four

Listen to the conversation and answer the questions. Put a circle round the letter of the correct answer. An example is done for you. *(20 seconds)* You will hear the conversation twice. You have two minutes to read through the questions below. *(2 minutes)*
[beep]
M: Judy Blume is the author of numerous books for readers of all ages, from picture books to middle grade and teen novels, to fiction for adults. Everyone is eager to learn about your new book, *Double Fudge.* Can you give us a hint as to what it's about?

W: In this book, five-year-old Fudge Hatcher becomes obsessed by money - he's drawing dollar signs at breakfast, thumbing through catalogues at bedtime, and making enough "Fudge Bucks" to buy the whole world - an embarrassment to his entire family, especially his older brother, Peter, who is just starting seventh grade. As if that weren't bad enough, the Hatchers meet up with their long lost (and eccentric) relatives, the Howie Hatchers of Honolulu, Hawaii, who happen to have twin daughters exactly Peter's age (who burst into song at the drop of a hat) plus a weird little boy. When Fudge discovers he's not the only Farley Drexel Hatcher in the world - well, you can imagine!

M: On your website - judyblume.com - you mention that your ten-year- old grandson Elliot was the inspiration for your new title. Does being a grandma give you a different perspective on childhood or children's literature? If so, how?

W: Being a grandparent is wonderful! I love it. But I don't think it gives me a different perspective on childhood or children's literature. It does help keep me in close touch with today's children. But I think most of us who write for children find ways of keeping in touch with the current generation. We're all observers. We all listen carefully. We're genuinely interested in kids. Otherwise we wouldn't write for and about them.

M: What is your writing process like?

W: I keep a notebook for months before I actually sit down to begin a new book. Before I start the notebook I have a vague idea of the characters and their story, usually something that's been brewing inside my head, sometimes for months, sometimes for years. I jot down anything that comes to mind during this period - details about characters, bits of dialogue, chapter ideas, descriptions - sometimes even scenes. This way, when I actually begin, I have my "security blanket". I find that when I'm doing a first draft it's important for me to keep going. Otherwise I get into revising each scene a million times and never move ahead. What works best for me is to get a first draft down as spontaneously as possible. It's very rough and I always think, if I die now this will never be published. No one will have a clue what it's about. I don't need to cool off between first and second drafts. A first draft for me is getting the pieces to the puzzle, the second draft is trying to make sense of the pieces, the third draft is painting a picture using the pieces, and all drafts after that are improving the picture. I like a cooling off period between the second and third drafts and again, before I send it to my editor. It's amazing how much you see when you've put the manuscript away for a couple of weeks, even a month. Then and this is so important, I'll read the manuscript out loud.

M: I guarantee, by reading and listening, you'll want to make so many changes.

W: A young novelist (two books published) was telling me recently that next time, he wants to record his book before it's copy edited. Me, too!

M: Many writers describe themselves as "character" or "plot" writers. Which are you? What do you think to be the hardest part of writing?

W: I'm a character writer but there wouldn't be a book if that character didn't have a story to tell. I tend to get ideas about a character in a situation. I don't like to think about "plot". I don't know everything that's going to happen when I begin. I know where I'm starting and where I'm hoping to wind up (though that sometimes changes along the way). The hardest part of writing for me is getting that first draft. I find it pure torture.

M: Adults lie to children or omit information all the time, yet you are forthright and honest through fiction. At first, was that a scary thing to do? Did you close your eyes and worry about irate grown-ups?

W: I didn't worry at all. I didn't even think about it. I was young and naive and nobody told me what I could or couldn't write. I was writing about what I knew to be true because I remembered it so clearly.

(Wait 10 seconds before repeating.) (10 seconds)

That is the end of Part Four. You now have two hours and forty minutes to complete the rest of the paper.

Test 2

Part one, part one

You will hear six short, unfinished conversations. Choose the **best reply** to continue each conversation. Put a circle round the letter of the **best reply**. Look at the example. *(15 seconds)* You will hear each conversation twice.

Number one. Number one. *(6 seconds)*

No.3 Audio Scripts

M: The interview went really well.

F: Oh, that's fantastic! I knew it would!

M: I doubt I'll get the job though.

(Wait 10 seconds before repeating.) (10 seconds)

Number two. Number two. *(6 seconds)*

F: You could have brought your children to the party.

M: I know; that wasn't the trouble.

F: Didn't you want to come?

(Wait 10 seconds before repeating.) (10 seconds)

Number three. Number three. *(6 seconds)*

F: How was Christmas with your family?

M: OK I guess. I hadn't seen my sister for years.

F: How are things between you two?

(Wait 10 seconds before repeating.) (10 seconds)

Number four. Number four. *(6 seconds)*

M: What happened with that important receipt?

F: Oh, eventually it turned up.

M: Where do you suppose they found it?

(Wait 10 seconds before repeating.) (10 seconds)

Number five. Number five. *(6 seconds)*

F: It certainly looks interesting...

M: Well, aren't you going to investigate further?

F: I'm not sure. There must be a catch.

(Wait 10 seconds before repeating.) (10 seconds)

Number six. Number six. *(6 seconds)*

M: I need the script for our holiday episode.

F: What? I thought Alison was responsible for that!

155

M: No, and you need to finish it by Friday!

(Wait 10 seconds before repeating.) (10 seconds)

That is the end of Part One.

Part two, part two

You will hear three conversations. Listen to the conversations and answer the questions. Put a circle round the letter of the correct answer. You will hear each conversation twice. Look at the questions for Conversation One. *(10 seconds)*

Conversation One

M: Hello Marge, do you think I could speak to you after class?

W: Sure, what about?

M: Just about your last paper. Don't worry, nothing is wrong. I was very impressed.

W: Did you grade it yet?

M: Yes, you got an A. I just wanted to see if you wanted to submit it to the school's literary journal. I really think it could get published.

W: Do you think so? Oh, I don't know. I've never had anything published!

M: There's a first time for everyone. I haven't read a paper this good all year. I think you have a lot of potential.

W: Thank you, that means so much coming from you. How do I go about submitting it?

M: That's what we'll talk about after class!

(Wait 10 seconds before repeating.) (10 seconds)

Now, look at the questions for Conversation Two. (10 seconds)

Conversation Two

W: Honey, I've been thinking about it a lot and I think you should open that pub you've been talking about.

M: Are you serious? I thought you said it was an awful idea and we'd lose a lot of money.

W: Well, maybe. But not if we do it right. And really, I just want you to be happy. And if opening up your own pub will make you happy then do it. But don't expect me to work there or really spend any time there.

M: Of course not, love, you won't even have to go in there if you don't want to! But this is a big decision, I mean, we're going to have to spend our savings on this.

W: I understand. But if you think it is a good idea, I'm behind you all the way.

(Wait 10 seconds before repeating.) (10 seconds)

Now, look at the questions for Conversation Three. (10 seconds)

Conversation Three

M: I'm so angry.

W: What happened?

M: Do you remember how hard I studied for my biology test last week?

W: Yes, you wouldn't even stop to get coffee with me. I've never seen anyone study so hard.

M: Well, I just got it back and I FAILED it. I mean, I did terribly. I don't know how it happened. I thought I knew everything and it turns out I knew NOTHING.

W: How could that possibly happen? Have you spoken to the professor?

M: No, and I haven't even seen the test, he just posted the grades outside his office.

W: Maybe there was a mistake. I think you should go make an appointment with him to discuss the test. And relax, one bad grade won't hurt you too much!

(Wait 10 seconds before repeating.) (10 seconds)

That is the end of Part Two.

Part three, part three

Listen to the person talking and complete the information on the notepad. Write short answers of one to five words. You will hear the person twice. At the end you will have two minutes to read through and check your answers. You have one minute to look at the notepad. The first one is an example. *(1 minute)*

[beep]

Good morning from Caitlin Butler on Mike and Lisa's Morning Radio Programme. I'm here today to talk about flowers and their enduring popularity as gifts, in addition to cross-cultural differences in flower - gifting. Doubtless most female listeners will have been the lucky recipient of a bouquet of flowers on more than one occasion in their lives. Flowers are a popular gift, and have been, since time immemorial. This is an indisputable fact. The reason being, flowers are universally acceptable and won't break the bank, even if you decide to splash out on more extravagant blooms to mark a special occasion. No matter the occasion, location or time, flowers are the perfect choice.

Before gifting flowers though, you would do well to have at least a passing knowledge of regional and cultural variations in flower-gifting patterns across the world, since any occasion worth its salt is invariably commemorated with flower-giving. Such variations have arisen out of a combination of both tradition and cultural belief systems that are firmly entrenched in all cultures.

In most cultures, virtually without exception, flowers are gifted at various rites of passage, like birthdays, weddings and anniversaries, funerals, to name but a few, as well as the popular occasions and festivals like Christmas, Mother's Day, Valentine's Day, etc. They are also popular as gifts even on formal occasions like Graduation day, Retirement day and even as casual gifts between friends, neighbours and colleagues as corporate gifts. Flowers are thus the most popular gift for any occasion. Globally, flowers invariably share a common symbolism throughout different cultures. Still, there do exist some regional and cultural variations in flower-gifting. For example, Peonies are the most popular flower gift in China, especially for weddings. However, potted plants are not appropriate as gifts in Asia. A plant symbolises that your relationship is restricted or bound up in a negative way and is therefore liable to inadvertently cause offence. Meanwhile, in Russia, birthday flower gifts are given as a single flower or a bunch. A floral arrangement or a floral gift basket are not usually chosen as a birthday gift in Russia. On Women's Day, Russians give red roses and spring flowers, such as tulips and hyacinths as well as solidago, which is the traditional flower for Women's Day. Moving onto English traditions now, it is common practice for guests to bring flowers when invited to someone's home. Beware of bringing white lilies, however, as they signify death and are more appropriate for funeral bouquets than festive occasions! Neither are red roses considered appropriate as a gift, unless one is declaring undying love to the intended recipient. In the UK, as in the rest of Europe, giving flowers in odd numbers is an old European tradition. The practice is still in vogue even today. But 13 flowers are never given, the number which is considered unlucky in the majority of European countries, unless of course you are in Italy, where the number 17 is considered to court bad luck.

So, as you can see, whilst flower-gifting is universally acceptable, there are many pitfalls associated with the practice. It is always better to familiarise yourself with cultural gift-giving practices and I mean, not only with regard to flower-giving, in order not to cause offence.

(Wait 10 seconds before repeating.) (10 seconds)

You will now have two minutes to read through and check your answers. (2 minutes) [beep]

That is the end of Part Three.

Part four, part four

Listen to the conversation and answer the questions. Put a circle round the letter of the correct answer. An example is done for you. *(20 seconds)* You will hear the conversation twice. You have two minutes to read through the questions below. *(2 minutes)*

[beep]

W: I've got to admit, Ben. I took this class about global warming but I still don't completely understand it. I mean, the teacher was good, still it was confusing.

M: Most people don't get it. It is a lot of information to process.

W: It isn't that it is too much to process, but everything is just too scientific. Could you explain it to me? I mean, I know some details, but the whole thing confuses me.

M: Of course I can. Okay, so to start, let's discuss the difference between El Nino and global warming. El Nino is a separate event from global warming, however there is a strong interaction between the ocean and the atmosphere through latent and sensible heat flux. So, if the atmosphere is getting warmer from global warming it makes sense that this would cause the ocean temperature to rise as well leading to a stronger El Nino.

W: Okay, so in your opinion, what needs to be done to avert the serious consequences of global warming? Like, if the atmosphere is getting warmer and that is a bad thing, how do we stop it?

M: There is now a very strong consensus among scientists that global warming is happening and something must be done about it. Although the burning of fossil fuels is the prime factor in global warming other activities such as deforestation and urbanisation are strong factors as well. Agriculture contributes a large amount of methane (a stronger greenhouse gas than CO_2). If we were to cap CO_2 emissions to 1990 levels that would be a significant improvement. A cap at 1985 levels would be even better. The problem though is the lag time. What we do now shows up in the atmosphere 10 years later and shows up in the ocean 20 years later, so even if we were to stop burning fossil fuels and deforestation today we would still see the effects of global warming increasing for another 20 years at least.

W: I heard that the scientists of the UN's IPCC said we need to cut emissions of CO_2 by 60% immediately if we are to avert catastrophe. In other words, it's going to get worse before it gets better no matter what we do but we still need to act as soon as possible if we care about future generations. That really scares me.

M: The U.S. has agreed to a 7% reduction from 1990 levels and is pushing the market solution of pollution certificate trading. It is unlikely though that this will achieve the necessary cut back in CO_2 to avoid disaster. The worst of these potential disasters is the phenomenon known as the runaway greenhouse effect. The runaway greenhouse effect is when the climate balance of the planet is pushed beyond the "point of no return". Venus has a runaway green house effect. The surface temperature is 700°C degrees, hot enough to melt lead. We don't know what the "point of no return" is for the Earth, but right now we are gambling with life on Earth. This is the same behaviour as a drug addict. Someone who keeps on smoking even though they know it's killing them. Except this time it's the entire planet that is at risk.

(Wait 10 seconds before repeating.) (10 seconds)

That is the end of Part Four. You now have two hours and forty minutes to complete the rest of the paper.

Test 3

Part one, part one

You will hear six short, unfinished conversations. Choose the **best reply** to continue each conversation. Put a circle round the letter of the **best reply**. Look at the example. *(15 seconds)* You will hear each conversation twice.

Number one. Number one. *(6 seconds)*

F: I didn't even ask Tom! Was that rude?

M: I thought you didn't get along; what are you worried about?

F: Did he want to come to our party too?

(Wait 10 seconds before repeating.) (10 seconds)

Number two. Number two. *(6 seconds)*

M: How was work?

F: Fine! Everything's back to normal.

M: So things sorted themselves out in the end?

(Wait 10 seconds before repeating.) (10 seconds)

Number three. Number three. *(6 seconds)*

F: That play we put on with the students was a lot of work!

M: I could tell they all had fun though.

F: What's your plan this week?

(Wait 10 seconds before repeating.) (10 seconds)

Number four. Number four. *(6 seconds)*

F: I heard you're moving to London.

M: Yes, I've been offered a very good position there.

F: Are you really going to do it?

(Wait 10 seconds before repeating.) (10 seconds)

Number five. Number five. *(6 seconds)*

M: Are you driving to France?

F: Yes, I can't wait! It's been years since I've gone!

M: Can I come along?

(Wait 10 seconds before repeating.) (10 seconds)

Number six. Number six. *(6 seconds)*

M: Did Justin ever turn up?

F: You don't like him, do you?

M: I'm just concerned. Did he?

(Wait 10 seconds before repeating.) (10 seconds)

That is the end of Part One.

Part two, part two

You will hear three conversations. Listen to the conversations and answer the questions. Put a circle round the letter of the correct answer. You will hear each conversation twice. Look at the questions for Conversation One. *(10 seconds)*

Conversation One

M: I'm so excited to come visit you!

W: I know, I can't wait! When will you be arriving?

M: I'm taking the train from here at 9 am so I'll be in the city by 3 at the latest. Then I have to switch trains and it is two hours after that. How about I'll call you at around 3 just to let you know where I'm at, but expect me there at 5 or 6.

W: Sounds great. Do you want me to meet you at the train station here?

M: That would be great. I've no idea where your new apartment is.

W: As long as you call me when you get close, I can take a taxi to the station.

(Wait 10 seconds before repeating.) (10 seconds)

Now, look at the questions for Conversation Two. (10 seconds)

Conversation Two

W: This was such a bad idea.

M: I know, I can't believe we chose this day to go to the beach.

W: Have you ever seen so much wind? Maybe we should just go home.

M: We drove three hours to get here, I don't want to go home.

W: Would you rather sit here in this terrible, cold, rainy, windy weather?

M: I guess not. We should have looked at the weather report before we left. What a waste of a Saturday.

W: Actually, I have an idea!

M: What's that?

W: Let's go out to eat. There are some pretty places along the water and it would be so nice to get some hot food in this bad weather.

M: That's a great idea, let's go.

(Wait 10 seconds before repeating.) (10 seconds)

Now, look at the questions for Conversation Three. (10 seconds)

Conversation Three

M: Hey! Sorry I'm so late!

W: Where were you? I've been worried sick!

M: Well, we went hiking, as you know, but we forgot to take a trail map which was a big mistake. Scott said he knew where we were going and we trusted him, but it turns out he doesn't have the best sense of direction in the world. Actually, he has a terrible sense of direction.

W: So what happened?

M: Well, we got about halfway up and we lost the trail and ended up walking around in circles for two hours before we found it again!

W: Bring your mobile next time you go hiking so I know you're not hurt when you're late!

(Wait 10 seconds before repeating.) (10 seconds)

That is the end of Part Two.

Part three, part three

Listen to the person talking and complete the information on the notepad. Write short answers of one to five words. You will hear the person twice. At the end you will have two minutes to read through and check your answers. You have one minute to look at the notepad. The first one is an example. *(1 minute)*

[beep]

Hello, my name is Ben and I'm here to talk to you about planning birthday celebrations for children. For many parents, planning a children's birthday party can prove a major headache, from organising and booking a suitable venue, to sending out invitations and buying party gifts. However, it needn't be like that. Of course, your child's birthday is a special day and needs celebrating as kids of all ages love to feel special on one day of the year. But children can be made to feel just as special on their birthday without all the unnecessary trappings and paraphernalia associated with most party events.

So, if your child's birthday party is days or weeks away from their actual birthday, or if you've decided to scrap the idea of a big birthday party altogether, there are lots of ways you can make your child feel special on their birthday. First of all, after your child goes to bed the night before their birthday, decorate the outside of their bedroom door with balloons, posters and stickers. When your child opens their bedroom door, they will be instantly greeted with the first reminder of their special day. This is as effective as it is simple to do. Another idea is, if your child is in school, take them to a restaurant and treat them to a slap-up breakfast in the morning and even let your child skip the first hour of the school day. The latter idea may even be more appreciated than the outing to the restaurant itself! Or, if you work and are pushed for time, make arrangements to pick your child up for lunch, taking an extended lunch hour if needs be and take your child out to their favourite restaurant. Also, don't forget that children love to be treated as grown-ups, once in a while. So let your child choose the birthday dinner menu for that night, too. Don't expect a grown-up menu, though! Adopt an "anything goes" policy. After all, your child only has a birthday once a year. So if your child fancies an overdose of carbs, pigging out on pizza, pasta and cake, then so be it! Don't forget to rave about how good his or her menu choices were! At the dinner table, for a conversation starter, have each family member share a funny story or a memory from the past about the birthday boy or girl. The most important thing to remember, is to offer your child a present that they will like and treasure for some time to come. Again, the present like the birthday preparations, does not have to be excessively expensive to please. Often even small gifts can be cherished if they reflect your child's interests or hobbies.

After dinner, is the best time to have the birthday cake, with all the singing and laughter that always goes with it. And that's probably the best time to offer your child the birthday present, which should be wrapped in nice paper. Kids always love surprises and the anticipation of unwrapping the present adds to the enjoyment of that special day. So I guess that just about wraps it up - if you'll pardon the pun! - for my advice on how to make your child's birthday just that extra bit special but without paying a fortune into the bargain! Trust me, if you follow these tips your child will have a birthday to remember!

(Wait 10 seconds before repeating.) (10 seconds)

You will now have two minutes to read through and check your answers. (2 minutes)

[beep]
That is the end of Part Three.

Part four, part four

Listen to the conversation and answer the questions. Put a circle round the letter of the correct answer. An example is done for you. *(20 seconds)* You will hear the conversation twice. You have two minutes to read through the questions below. *(2 minutes)*

[beep]

I: Hello! Today we're talking to Meryl Jones about her newest movie "Hello Mama!" I gather that when you saw the show on Broadway you sent a "well done" letter to the cast of the musical. Was that your way of saying count me in if there's a movie?

M.J.: I did see the show and I did write a note many years ago to the cast of the Broadway production. I saw it in New York and I took my 10-year-old for her birthday party. It was right after it had opened and it was right after September 11th 2001 and everyone was feeling really low. And I thought: "What am I going to do with all these kids?" And I saw an ad in the *NY Times* and it said: "New British musical - buoyant fun:" and I thought, "I'm there!" So, I took the kids and we were all dancing in the aisles and down the street- we bought the cast album and sang the songs for two years. And so that's why I wrote the note to the cast, to basically say: *"Thank You For The Music* and for the injection of joy that was so needful at that moment."

I: How difficult was it to begin a song in London and finish it in Greece?

M.J.: Well, I think I've sung all of these songs about 50,000 times! From starting in my closet - which was the only place my family would allow me to practise - all the way to London. I never got sick of singing these songs, never ever. In my dance school they used to use '*The Rockies*' songs to rev everybody up for dance class because you just can't not be excited when it starts. So, it wasn't a big problem re-inserting yourself into the moment, from London to Greece. Greece was just nicer.

I: How much influence did George and James, the producers and founders of the group *'The Rockies'* have in the way you performed the songs?

M.J.: They were there all the time, whenever we were recording. First we did a pre-record and then we recorded on body mikes while we were shooting. They were very generous in how they let us own the songs and express their songs, as long as we were exact on the words and the timing. I didn't want to disappoint them, or let them down. But there are so many great songs and it was such a joy to sing them. It wasn't hard work.

I: This was quite a physical role. Did you do all your own stunts - singing as well as dancing?

M.J.: Of course. The hardest number was *My Heart Goes.* It was so hard to learn those dance steps. We worked on it for three weeks before shooting and it was everyone's bette noir, all the non-dancing actors, which is to basically say all the actors, apart from Helen. I don't think there's a single shot of our feet in that sequence. It went so fast and there were 150 people on set, it's the only number where everybody was dancing at once, the whole cast and every dancer in London I think. It was really scary. And then there were those disco lights, eight hours a day - we couldn't wait to get there in the morning to do it again, right?

I: How did you go about creating such a close bond with your fellow cast members?

M.J.: People who work on plays have this experience but most movies people fly in and do their bit and then fly out again. But on this, because we were incarcerated in that barn trying to learn *My Heart Goes* for three weeks before filming started, all we thought about was *My Heart Goes,* we didn't have time to worry about anything else. Colin Stein was so worried about it and Keith Brown was beside himself, Harry Newton was drenched in sweat every day, but we all bonded over that. We felt like a company and we lived together. That's a large part of why we were able to bond so well. And then, of course, we went to Greece and were in the most beautiful place!

(Wait 10 seconds before repeating.)

(10 seconds)

That is the end of Part Four.

You now have two hours and forty minutes to complete the rest of the paper.

Test 4

Part one, part one

You will hear six short, unfinished conversations. Choose the **best reply** to continue each conversation. Put a circle round the letter of the **best reply**. Look at the example. *(15 seconds)* You will hear each conversation twice.

Number one. Number one. *(6 seconds)*

F: There's Amy; poor thing!

M: Has something happened?

F: Didn't you hear?

(Wait 10 seconds before repeating.) (10 seconds)

Number two. Number two. *(6 seconds)*

F: I have to baby-sit my younger brother tonight.

M: So you are going to miss the fireworks?

F: Yes; will you be there?

(Wait 10 seconds before repeating.) (10 seconds)

Number three. Number three. *(6 seconds)*

F: Were the posters effective?

M: They must have been; the seats have already sold out!

F: How many tickets did you make available?

(Wait 10 seconds before repeating.) (10 seconds)

Number four. Number four. *(6 seconds)*

F: Did you choose your flight?

M: I can't come home for Easter, Mum, I have to study.

F: This is such a shock.

(Wait 10 seconds before repeating.) (10 seconds)

Number five. Number five. *(6 seconds)*

F: Are you waiting to be interviewed too?

M: Yes. Oh, excuse me! They're calling me in!

F: I hope things go well for you.

(Wait 10 seconds before repeating.) (10 seconds)

Number six. Number six. *(6 seconds)*

F: Where's Julie?

M: Oh, didn't you know? She left.

F: When did that happen?

(Wait 10 seconds before repeating.) (10 seconds)

That is the end of Part One.

Part two, part two

You will hear three conversations. Listen to the conversations and answer the questions. Put a circle round the letter of the correct answer. You will hear each conversation twice. Look at the questions for Conversation One. *(10 seconds)*

Conversation One

W: You want to leave on August 1st? That might be difficult.

M: I know, we really should have come in here sooner. It just took us a while to figure out when we were all free. We'll take any ferry, any time of day, it really doesn't matter.

W: Here's one that leaves at 9 pm and it arrives on the island at 3 am. Does that work?

M: What are we supposed to do when we get there? Sleep on the street? Do you have anything else?

W: We have an overnight one with cabins available. You'd leave at 8 pm and arrive at 6:30 am.

M: And what about for our return?

W: What day will you be returning?

M: The 10th of August.

W: We have a highspeed boat at 2 pm that arrives at 7 pm that same evening. Does that sound good?

M: Do you have one earlier in the morning?

W: We have one that leaves at 8 am and arrives at 1 pm. Does that work?

M: Perfect.

W: And what about hotel accommodation? Are you OK with that?

M: Yes, we're actually staying with friends. Thank you so much, I'll be in to pick up the tickets tomorrow.

(Wait 10 seconds before repeating.) (10 seconds)
Now, look at the questions for Conversation Two. (10 seconds)

Conversation Two

W: What a lovely place. I want to try the lobster.

M: I'm glad you like it. I made reservations over a month ago.

W: What's the occasion? You're lucky I wasn't busy!

M: I just hoped you weren't! And besides, you spend every Saturday with me anyway!

W: That's true. So what are you going to order?

M: I was thinking the steak. We might as well indulge while we're here!

W: Not seafood? They have fresh Atlantic Salmon.

M: Ooohhh I didn't even see that. And look at this, they have scallops! My favourite. I'll have to order that.

W: That's more like the man I know. I've never seen you order steak before.

M: Well, we're at such a fancy place, I felt like it was appropriate. But you're right, seafood is more my thing.

(Wait 10 seconds before repeating.) (10 seconds)
Now, look at the questions for Conversation Three. (10 seconds)

Conversation Three

M: Excuse me, how many people can sleep comfortably in this tent?

W: It says three on the label, but with all your gear I'd say only two people would be comfortable in it.

M: Do you have anything larger? My three friends and I are going camping next week and we need a tent.

W: We have this one here.

M: Yes, I saw that, but it seems to be taller and not any wider.

W: It means you can stand!

M: But I don't want to stand, I want to fit four people in a tent.

W: I'd really recommend just buying two of these. You'll be much more comfortable. And also, remember to buy a tarp and a rain cover.

M: Okay, I'll take your advice. Also, do you have hiking shoes for sale in here?

W: Yes, go to the back of the store and someone there will be able to help you out.

(Wait 10 seconds before repeating.) (10 seconds)

That is the end of Part Two.

Part three, part three

Listen to the person talking and complete the information on the notepad. Write short answers of one to five words. You will hear the person twice. At the end you will have two minutes to read through and check your answers. You have one minute to look at the notepad. The first one is an example. *(1 minute)*

[beep]

Choosing the right tent is vital when it comes to the Great Outdoors. Inclement weather can jeopardise any camping expedition, irrespective of how experienced a camper may be. At best, waterlogged provisions and clothing can dampen the camping experience, in more ways than one and at worst, can result in cold-induced flu or even pneumonia in a worst case scenario. It is better to be prepared therefore than suffer the consequences of having inadequate camping equipment. So, when choosing a tent, there is no better choice than The North Face VE 25.

The North Face VE 25 is a spectacular tent suitable for all occasions. Excellent for four-season use and any outdoor adventure that requires hunkering down in inhospitable conditions. The North Face VE 25 is the most popular expedition tent made by The North Face. With a trail weight of 9 lbs., 12 oz., it's substantially lighter than most tents in the expedition line. No need therefore to sacrifice warmth, by limiting your warm clothes in order to have a lighter load. No need to ditch your favourite woolly jumper or extra pair of walking shoes! You can have it all with the North Face VE 25! Not only will you be travelling light but you will also have a tent where you can have room to stretch out after a long and tiring day. The North Face VE 25 offers considerably more space than the two-person Mountain 25 tent.

If you are a seasoned or just an amateur mountaineer, being able to capitalise on the extra space available in the North Face VE 25 tent is vital when waiting out a storm and sheltering from the wind and rain. In addition, like many of the best-designed mountaineering tents, the VE 25 has an integrated polyurethane view window that's cold tested to －60° F so you can check on the weather without compromising any of the warmth inside the tent. This is an important consideration, since losing heat and body warmth as a result, can put you at risk of hypothermia with potentially fatal consequences. If on the other hand, weather conditions are not adverse and it begins to get too muggy inside the tent, unzip the adjustable mesh vents for bug-free cross ventilation. After all, there is nothing worse than spending the night with a mosquito buzzing incessantly around your head!

With the North Face VE 25, you can also sleep-easy as the guy-out points are numerous enough to weather big blows. In addition, the no-stretch Kevlar guylines with camping adjustments are ideal for pitching in open spaces so you'll be spoilt for choice when it comes to positioning your tent. Finally, the VE 25 comes with internal storage pockets for gear, but if you really want to organise (and possibly dry out) your mountaineering and backpacking gear, get the fully-compatible GL 25X. This is the perfect additional component, as it will give you the extra storage space you need for those essential items that you can't leave home without!

Adaptable, safe, comfortable and suitable for all weather, the North Face VE 25 is the tent for any would-be or seasoned camper. Available now in selected stores and online!

(Wait 10 seconds before repeating.) (10 seconds)

You will now have two minutes to read through and check your answers. (2 minutes)

[beep]

That is the end of Part Three.

Part four, part four

Listen to the conversation and answer the questions. Put a circle round the letter of the correct answer. An example is done for you. *(20 seconds)* You will hear the conversation twice. You have two minutes to read through the questions below. *(2 minutes)*

[beep]

W: Today we're talking with Mr. Jeff Galloway, best-selling author, Olympic athlete, *Runners World* columnist, and creator of the Galloway RUN-WALK Method. He has a brand new book: *Galloway's 5K/10K Running.* So, Mr. Galloway, you've written several books about running, and you were a 1972 Olympic athlete. What was your race?

M: I made the team in the 10,000 metres run and was an alternate marathoner.

W: How did you begin running?

M: As a 13-year-old kid, I was fat and sedentary. In school we were required to participate in a sport. I chose winter track conditioning because I heard it was the easiest. Fortunately, after hiding out in the woods for part of practice, I fell into a group of kids who liked to run.

W: What is the Galloway Run-Walk method that teaches almost anyone how to complete a marathon?

M: In 1974, I began to teach a community class on beginning running at Florida State University. No one in class had run for at least five years. I divided the participants into groups: beginners walking with breaks, more advanced running with walking breaks, and the most advanced group, fewest walking breaks. All finished either a 5 thousand metres or a 10 thousand metres race without injuries. This is rare. The walk-breaks allowed them to remain injury-free. Walk-breaks need to come before people become tired. More than 200,000 people over the years have successfully used this method. I have also designed a whole system, incorporating a "magic mile", which is a timed mile. The time is converted to a slow training pace; when followed this means no injuries should occur.

W: Is running good for anyone?

M: Practically anyone can walk and run. Our ancestors had to run and walk to survive; it was their means of transportation to the next food supply. The constant movement and migration in small groups developed the human traits of teamwork. They were long distance athletes; we are genetically endowed to be able to run. Psychological studies have shown that brain development due to aerobic activity, makes the thinking process more direct and efficient; running enhances the ability to use the brain better. Runners have the highest positive attitude traits and the least amounts of depression. Other studies have shown that physical or chemical changes occur after beginning running. You just feel good.

W: Mr. Galloway, your books are the current best sellers for running. Tell me about them.

M: I've written ten books, two about walking and eight about running, specifically marathons. My original publication, *Galloway's Book on Running,* has sold over 600,000 copies, and is the current best seller of all running books. My recent publications are focused on women - *The Women's Complete Guide to Running,* and *The Women's Complete Guide to Walking.*

(Wait 10 seconds before repeating.) (10 seconds)

No.3 Audio Scripts

That is the end of Part Four. You now have two hours and forty minutes to complete the rest of the paper.

Test 5

Part one, part one

You will hear six short, unfinished conversations. Choose the **best reply** to continue each conversation. Put a circle round the letter of the **best reply**. Look at the example. *(15 seconds)* You will hear each conversation twice.

Number one. Number one. *(6 seconds)*

F: What a vile smell! You left food in a borrowed tent?

M: Yep. And attracted a skunk.

F: How are you going to explain that?

(Wait 10 seconds before repeating.) (10 seconds)

Number two. Number two. *(6 seconds)*

M: You've had your hair cut; it looks great!

F: Uh, I've had this haircut for ages, Tim.

M: Wasn't it done recently?

(Wait 10 seconds before repeating.) (10 seconds)

Number three. Number three. *(6 seconds)*

F: This furniture was your own design?

M: Yes, and I built it all from scratch, too.

F: You should feel so proud!

(Wait 10 seconds before repeating.) (10 seconds)

Number four. Number four. *(6 seconds)*

M: What do you reckon? The pepperoni?

173

F: I don't want anything heavy; I'd prefer the garden pizza.

M: Maybe we could get half pepperoni and half garden.

(Wait 10 seconds before repeating.) (10 seconds)

Number five. Number five. *(6 seconds)*

F: Why the long face?

M: I can't face another day; I'm going to shout at my manager.

F: What're the issues you're having?

(Wait 10 seconds before repeating.) (10 seconds)

Number six. Number six. *(6 seconds)*

F: I think we'd better fill up the car here.

M: But the tank's still half full.

F: It may be a while till the next town though.

(Wait 10 seconds before repeating.) (10 seconds)

That is the end of Part One.

Part two, part two

You will hear three conversations. Listen to the conversations and answer the questions. Put a circle round the letter of the correct answer. You will hear each conversation twice. Look at the questions for Conversation One. *(10 seconds)*

Conversation One

W: Tell me again, what type of medicine do you practise?

M: Ayurvedic medicine. It is basically ancient Indian medicine, but it can certainly still be applied today.

W: What are the basics of it?

M: Basically, the human body can be broken down into elements: earth, fire, air and water. When someone is sick it means the balance of those elements is off. For example, if you have a fever, you have too much of the fire element in you. Certain herbs and foods can heal this.

W: What about serious illness, like cancer?

No.3 Audio Scripts

M: Of course, Ayurvedic medicine doesn't have all the answers, but I recommend a mix of Western and Ayurvedic medicine. Sometimes one is better, sometimes the other is better.

W: That's fascinating. I'd like to learn more about it.

M: I'm giving a lecture on my job to a group of students tomorrow if you'd like to stop by and listen.

(Wait 10 seconds before repeating.) (10 seconds)

Now, look at the questions for Conversation Two. (10 seconds)

Conversation Two

W: Do you like these shoes I've just bought?

M: I don't know, they're fine I guess.

W: I just bought them, they're supposed to be good for my feet, and since I'm standing up all day at work I thought it would be a good idea to have a comfortable pair of shoes. The trouble is, even though they're very comfortable in some respect, the strap rubs against my toe and I can't stand it.

M: Doesn't that usually happen when you get new shoes? It takes a while to break them in.

W: Well sure but usually I get uncomfortable high heels and of course that happens with them; but these shoes are supposed to be comfortable.

M: Well, can you return them?

W: No.

M: Oh, just try wearing them for a week or so and see what happens. I hope they'll be fine after a few days.

(Wait 10 seconds before repeating.) (10 seconds)

Now, look at the questions for Conversation Three. (10 seconds)

Conversation Three

M: What else do we need to buy for this party?

W: Food. We haven't even gone grocery shopping yet. I can't believe we only have four more hours. We're never going to be ready on time.

M: Relax, we don't even have much to do. The house is decorated, everyone is going to be here at 6, Jim is picking up Linda at the airport. It will work out. She's going to be so surprised.

W: I can't believe she's coming home! I'm so excited and nervous! It has been 6 months since we've seen her. Can you believe it? I hope she likes the party!

M: Relax. Just relax. Why don't you stay here and take a nap and I'll go to get the food. Okay? Everything is going to be just fine.

W: I can't take a nap I have to get her bedroom ready. But I will let you go out and get the food. At least I won't have to worry about that.

(Wait 10 seconds before repeating.) (10 seconds)

That is the end of Part Two.

Part three, part three

Listen to the person talking and complete the information on the notepad. Write short answers of one to five words. You will hear the person twice. At the end you will have two minutes to read through and check your answers. You have one minute to look at the notepad. The first one is an example. *(1 minute)*

[beep]

Ernest Miller Hemingway was born on July 21st, 1899 in Oak Park, Illinois, a suburb of Chicago. Hemingway was the first son and the second child born to Clarence Edmonds "Doc Ed" Hemingway - a country doctor, and Grace Hall Hemingway. The Hemingways lived in a six-bedroom Victorian house built by Ernest's widowed maternal grandfather, Ernest Miller Hall, an English immigrant and Civil War veteran who lived with the family. Author Hemingway, was Earnest Hall's namesake.

Ernest Hemingway was a novelist, short-story writer, and journalist who started his career as a writer in a newspaper office in Kansas City at the age of seventeen. He was part of the 1920s expatriate community in Paris, later known as *"the Lost Generation"*. He lived there for a number of years, and was one of the veterans of World War I. During the War he had joined as a volunteer in the ambulance unit in the Italian army. Serving at the front, he was wounded and then decorated by the Italian Government; he spent considerable time in hospitals.

During the twenties, Hemingway became a member of the group of expatriate Americans in Paris, which he described in his first important work, *The Sun Also Rises* (1926).

Equally successful was *A Farewell to Arms* (1929), the study of an American ambulance officer's disillusionment in the war and his role as a deserter. Hemingway used his experiences as a reporter during the civil war in Spain as the background for his most ambitious novel, *For Whom the Bell Tolls* (1940). Among his later works, the most outstanding is the short novel, *The Old Man and the Sea,* for which Hemingway received the Pulitzer Prize in 1953 and the Nobel Prize in Literature in 1954.

Ernest Hemingway is truly an iconic figure, a man who lived large on the world's stage. Not just his writing, but his lifestyle too has become the stuff of legend, a willing ambassador for the *Lost Generation,* the globetrotting, prize-winning author, cavorted with Hollywood stars, tracked game through the African bush, fished the Gulf Stream, survived two plane crashes, and once even hunted German U-boats in the Caribbean. Hemingway's distinctive writing style is characterised by economy and understatement, and had a significant influence on the development of twentieth-century fiction writing. His protagonists are typically stoical men who exhibit an ideal described as "grace under pressure". Many of his works are now considered classics of American literature.

The influence of Hemingway's writings on American literature was considerable and continues today. James Joyce called *A Clean, Well-Lighted Place* "one of the best stories ever written". The same story also influenced several of Edward Hopper's best known paintings, most notably *Nighthawks.* Pulp fiction and "hard-boiled" crime fiction (which flourished from the 1920s to the 1950s) often owed a strong debt to Hemingway. Hemingway attempted suicide in the spring of 1961, and received ECT treatment again. On the morning of July 2nd, 1961, some three weeks short of his 62nd birthday, he died at his home in Ketchum, Idaho, as the result of a self-inflicted shotgun wound to the head. Judged not mentally responsible for his final act, he was buried in a Roman Catholic service.

(Wait 10 seconds before repeating.) (10 seconds)

You will now have two minutes to read through and check your answers. (2 minutes)

[beep]

That is the end of Part Three.

Part four, part four

Listen to the conversation and answer the questions. Put a circle round the letter of the correct answer. An example is done for you. *(20 seconds)* You will hear the conversation twice. You have two minutes to read through the questions below. *(2 minutes)*

[beep]

W: Here you are, John Smith, whom not only for me, but for most of those who write serious film criticism, or make movies, considered as possibly the number-one living filmmaker, both in the importance of the body of your work and in your influence on other filmmakers.

M: And here is what you are to me: in addition to being a great filmmaker who has forged ahead in an area where you are practically unique, that is, the diary, journal film, you are the only one who has created a believable, meaningful, extended journal across most of your adult life. In addition to this, you have found a way to sponsor films that you love and to create cooperatives through which they can be distributed; to create Anthology Film Archives so that they could be preserved and shown in a repertoire and continue today to be certainly the only place for what we want to call Poetic Film. So, you have not only done these two things, but you also have this rich life as a poet. Not knowing Lithuanian, I can just read the English translations of your works, which are very moving to me. I don't know how you keep all this going.

W: We have both been in it all for fifty years now. You have been making films since 1953. And me, in the Spring of 1953 I moved to the Lower East Side of New York and opened my first showcase for the avant garde films at the Gallery East. I showed Kenneth Anger, Gregory Markopoulos, Maya Deren, and Sidney Peterson. So you see, I didn't move very far.

M: Well, the person who really gets something done is the one who can stay at home! Of course, ironically, you are an exile, exiled from your home.

W: We lived in a century where for maybe half the world it was made impossible to remain at home. So now, I often say that cinema is my home. I used to say culture was my home. But it got a little bit confused. Nobody knows what culture is anymore. So I stick to cinema.

M: That's where you and I got into trouble, with what culture was and art. I was so frightened the social concerns of the sixties would overwhelm the long-range aesthetic possibilities, as I viewed them. As I look back on it now, I think that you were largely right, that I needn't have been afraid for the arts in the ways in which I was. Let's say, many of the films that came out were very stupid from a standpoint of art, or aesthetics or even craftsmanship. Still, they were crucial to the moment.

W: When we celebrated Anthology Film Archives 30th anniversary, I got together with Ken Kelman and P. Adams Sitney and we talked about the creation of the Essential Cinema Repertory, which consisted of some 330 titles of very carefully selected films that we felt indicated the perimeters of the art of cinema. We came to the conclusion that we did not make any bad mistakes in our choices. I discovered that what I showed, what I promoted, all ended up in the Essential Cinema Repertory, the films that are now considered the classics of the sixties. There were, of course, some that did not become classics. Important works are always surrounded by some that are not that important, but as time goes by they fall off. In a sense, it's like Darwin's law applied to the arts. Not the biggest, but the most essential survive.

M: I was afraid the lesser works would sink the ship.

W: They just evaporate. Your work, or that of Kenneth Anger, Maya Deren, and Michael Snow, they just keep growing.

M: But I also wonder if that doesn't have more to do with what you provided.

W: What came up during my conversation with P. Adams Sitney, was that what's lacking today is serious or passionate writing on the contemporary avant garde film. That, of course, was my function in the Village Voice, via my column Movie Journal.

(Wait 10 seconds before repeating.) (10 seconds)

That is the end of Part Four. You now have two hours and forty minutes to complete the rest of the paper.

About LanguageCert English Spoken Other Language（ESOL）Test

LanguageCert 考试

分为 LanguageCert ESOL Online、LanguageCert ESOL 以及 LanguageCert ESOL SELT 三种类型。

LanguageCert ESOL Online

可以通过官网 languagecert.org 或者使用微信扫描以下小程序码进行考试报名。

LanguageCert ESOL

需要通过线下授权考试中心进行报名。如果您需要了解当地考试中心的联系方式，可以使用微信扫描小程序码，随后联系在线客服获取距您最近的考试中心的联系方式。

LanguageCert ESOL SELT

SELT 考试需要在 languagecert.org 进行考试预约以及报名。如果想要进一步地了解情况，请您联系小程序的在线客服。

Answer Key

Test 1

Listening Part 1
1.a 2.a 3.b 4.c 5.c 6.a

Listening Part 2
1.a 2.b 3.c 4.a 5.c 6.c

Listening Part 3
1. the Soviet Union - the USA
2. Nicaragua
3. The Enterprise
4. (the secrecy) of US government
5. (the) overthrow of its/Guatemala's ruler
6. the market in fruit exports
7. the Watergate (scandal)

Listening Part 4
1.c 2.a 3.c 4.c 5.b 6.a 7.c

Reading Part 1
1.T 2.T 3.T 4.F 5.F

Reading Part 2
1.H 2.A 3.C 4.G 5.B 6.D

Reading Part 3
1.C 2.B 3.A 4.D 5.C 6.A 7.B

Reading Part 4
1.(it is) highly problematic/challenging
2.a variety of mental tests
3.the "lateral prefrontal cortex"
4.(a function of) social factors (such as education)
5.(in the) seventeenth century
6.(those children) with learning difficulties
7.mental ability
8.(our) social background

Test 2

Listening Part 1
1.b 2.c 3.c 4.b 5.c 6.a

Listening Part 2
1.a 2.a 3.a 4.a 5.c 6.b

Listening Part 3
1. tradition and cultural belief systems

Test 3

2. Christmas / Mother's Day / Valentine's Day
3. Graduation Day / Retirement Day
4. China
5. potted plants
6. white lilies
7. seventeen /17

Listening Part 4

1.b 2.a 3.a 4.a 5.a 6.b 7.b

Reading Part 1

1.T 2.F 3.T 4.F 5.F

Reading Part 2

1.G 2.E 3.B 4.A 5.D 6.H

Reading Part 3

1.C 2.B 3.A 4.D 5.C 6.A 7.B

Reading Part 4

1. the feeling of performing / the Instrument Game Controller
2. from 1700s to 1930s
3. that it impacts on culture / (being) a platform for cultural dialogue
4. the French horn
5. the synchronicity of the orchestra/ensemble
6. (the most) musically conservative (ever)
7. controversial
8. (it engaged) a new audience

Listening Part 1

1.a 2.c 3.c 4.a 5.a 6.a

Listening Part 2

1.a 2.a 3.c 4.c 5.a 6.a

Listening Part 3

1. the night before (their/child's) birthday
2. balloons / posters / stickers
3. breakfast
4. the dinner menu
5. (his/her) menu choices
6. share a story/memory
7. after dinner

Listening Part 4

1.a 2.a 3.c 4.a 5.a 6.b 7.a

Reading Part 1

1.F 2.F 3.T 4.T 5.T

Reading Part 2

1.H 2.A 3.C 4.G 5.B 6.D

Reading Part 3

1.C 2.A 3.B 4.D 5.C 6.A 7.B

Reading Part 4

1. in London
2. few records survive
3. The (Romantics) (and the) Victorians admired him
4. his plays are consistently performed
5. cultural and political
6. for mixing comic and tragic
7. classical ideas were in vogue
8. his 'primitiveness'

Test 4

Listening Part 1

1.a 2.c 3.b 4.a 5.a 6.a

Listening Part 2

1.c 2.b 3.b 4.c 5.a 6.a

Listening Part 3

1. North Face VE25
2. Expedition
3. 9 lbs, 12 oz
4. Two-person Mountain 25
5. — 60 degrees F
6. GL25X
7. in selected stores and/or online

Listening Part 4

1.a 2.a 3.c 4.b 5.a 6.a 7.a

Reading Part 1

1.F 2.F 3.T 4.T 5.T

Reading Part 2

1.C 2.A 3.H 4.D 5.G 6.F

Reading Part 3

1.A 2.C 3.B 4.D 5.C 6.B 7.A

Reading Part 4

1. to amalgamate society / the Revolution War ended
2. to form propaganda / to convince/ persuade New York citizens
3. as a sensible decision / as a logical choice
4. factions / segmented communities
5. to regulate/control their effects/influence
6. that factions are regulated / the issue of property rights
7. to allow governmental self-regulation
8. it will protect their/individual rights

Test 5

Listening Part 1

1.a 2.c 3.c 4.a 5.a 6.a

Listening Part 2

1.a 2.b 3.c 4.c 5.a 6.a

Listening Part 3

1. July 21st, 1899
2. Paris
3. the Lost Generation
4. 1953
5. Literature
6. 20th-century fiction (writing)
7. (committed) suicide

Listening Part 4

1.a 2.a 3.c 4.a 5.a 6.a 7.a

Reading Part 1

1.T 2.T 3.T 4.F 5.F

Reading Part 2

1.H 2.A 3.G 4.C 5.B 6.D

Reading Part 3

1.C 2.B 3.A 4.C 5.D 6.B 7.A

Reading Part 4

1. it unites two sides (East and West) / the Prime Meridian is (located) there / home of Greenwich Mean Time
2. to guide ships / to improve navigation at sea
3. providing the skies' precise chart/ the accurate measurment of time
4. standing on the equator
5. in 1850
6. time has a co-ordinate base/ world times were-coordinated
7. by the Prime Meridan
8. convenience